LORD HAℕ
TWILIGHT OVER
ENGLAND

WILLIAM JOYCE

Ostara Publications

Lord Haw-Haw: Twilight over England

By William Joyce Aka "Lord Haw-Haw"

First published 1940 as "Twilight over England"

By the Internationaler Verlag, Berlin

This edition

2015

Ostara Publications

http://ostarapublications.com

ISBN 978-1-64606-569-1

Contents

William Joyce and his wife in Germany during World War II.

William Joyce: A Short Biography

William Joyce was born in New York of an Irish father and an English mother on April 24, 1906. When he was three, his family moved to Ireland, settling in County Mayo.

Joyce was educated at the College of St. Ignatius Loyola Galway. In 1921, the Joyce family moved to England. By this time, the 15-year-old Joyce was a strapping youngster, excelling at boxing, swimming, and fencing. His political views were also entirely formed by this age, and when he was 17, he joined the 'British Fascisti'—Britain's first fascist movement, modeled on the Italian original.

In 1924, while attending a Conservative meeting at Lambeth Bath Hall, Joyce and some fellow Fascisti were attacked by Communist thugs. In the fight which followed, a Communist, who Joyce later said had a "Jewish face," slashed him with a knife. This serious wound left a deep scar on the right side of his face from the lobe of his ear to the corner of his mouth.

By 1925, Joyce had resigned from the British Fascisti. Politically adrift, he joined the Conservative Party in 1931, but left after a short time in disgust.

When Sir Oswald Mosley launched the British Union of Fascists (BUF) on October 1, 1932, Joyce rushed to join. His activism and excellent public speaking ability made him highly popular and by 1934, he had been appointed the BUF's Director of Propaganda.

Later that same year, he was appointed Deputy Leader of the BUF, directly under Mosley. The two men were however polar opposites in character, and clashed frequently. Finally, in 1937, when the BUF was forced to reduce its salaried staff from 143 to 30, the position of deputy leader was one of those excised, and Joyce left the movement.

Never one to be halted, Joyce went straight on to found the British National Socialist League (BNSL), taking about 60 members with him. Although small in comparison to the BUF, the BNSL was highly active and of far greater concern to the Jewish establishment than the Mosley movement.

His dedication to National Socialism and his understanding of the forces at work in Europe allowed Joyce to understand perfectly well that by 1939, war would be inevitable. As a result, on August 26, 1939, just a week before the war started, he and his family left Britain after a tip-off that, under the soon to be introduced emergency powers, he would be interned by the "democratic" British government.

Once in Germany, Joyce's long-established contacts enabled his appointment as editor and speaker for the German transmitters for Europe, based in Berlin. It was these wartime broadcasts to England which earned him his greatest fame. The name "Lord Haw-Haw of Zeesen" was actually coined in 1939 by a *Daily Express* radio critic to refer to another German radio announcer, Wolf Mittler.

When Joyce became the best-known German radio propaganda broadcaster, the "Lord Haw-Haw" nickname was transferred to him, and not, as many historians have alleged, because of a supposed "aristocratic sounding nasal drawl" supposedly acquired as a result of boyhood fist-fight.

Initially Joyce preferred to be an anonymous broadcaster, but his increasing popularity and listenership in Britain finally persuaded him to use his real name. Joyce had an estimated six million regular and 18 million occasional listeners in the United Kingdom—almost as many listeners as the BBC.

For his efforts Joyce was awarded the Cross of War Merit 1st Class with a certificate signed by Adolf Hitler, although they never met in person.

As the war turned against Germany, Joyce moved to Hamburg, where, on the evening of April 30, 1945, he made his last broadcast as British troops were entering the city. A National Socialist to the last, he signed off for the last time with a defiant "Heil Hitler."

Joyce was captured while walking through a wood on May 28, 1945, by a group of British soldiers.

After speaking to him in French and English, they asked Joyce if he was Lord Haw-Haw. Joyce had a prepared forged passport in his pocket under another name, but as he reached into his coat to get it, the soldiers—presuming he was going for a weapon—opened fire, wounding him in his lower torso.

He was arrested, and shipped back to London for trial on charges of treason. His trial quickly became a farce after it emerged that he had been born in America, and was actually of Irish nationality. It was true that he had applied for a British passport in 1936, but in that application, Joyce had lied and said that he was a British citizen.

According to the law, an application for a passport made with false information invalidated the passport, so, strictly legally speaking, Joyce never had a valid British passport, and was therefore never a British citizen, and could consequently not be charged with treason towards a country of whom he had never been a national.

The possibility of an acquittal seemed to be the only outcome, but the British Attorney General, Sir Hartley Shawcross, launched a personal appeal to the court, arguing that Joyce's possession of a British passport, even though he had misstated his nationality to get it, entitled him (until it expired, on July 2, 1940) to British diplomatic protection in Germany and therefore he owed allegiance to the king at the time he commenced working for the Germans.

On this highly dubious basis—unfounded in terms of British citizenship acquisition laws—Joyce was convicted of treason and sentenced to death on September 19, 1945.

He immediately appealed, arguing that possession of a passport did not entitle him to the protection of the Crown, and that jurisdiction had been wrongly assumed by the court in putting on trial an alien for offences committed in a foreign country.

This argument was rejected by the appeal court on the highly questionable and extremely legally dubious basis that a "state may exercise such jurisdiction in the interests of its own security."

By now it was clear that no matter what the legal situation, the establishment sought Joyce's death. All of his legal avenues exhausted, he was hanged on January 3, 1946, at Wandsworth Prison, aged 39.

He was buried in an unmarked grave within the walls of the prison, but in 1976, his remains were exhumed and reinterred in the New Cemetery in Galway, Ireland, where he had grown up.

AUTHOR'S PREFACE

THE preface is usually that part of a book which can most safely be omitted. It usually represents that efflorescent manifestation of egotism which an author, after working hard, cannot spare either himself or his readers. More often than not the readers spare themselves.

When, however, the writer is a daily perpetrator of High Treason, his introductory remarks may command from the English public that kind of awful veneration with which £5000 confessions are perused in the Sunday newspapers, quite frequently after the narrator has taken his last leap in the dark.

At any rate, I have reason to believe that many fictitious stories are being circulated about me in England already: and it seems less than fair to neglect to provide them with that basis of fact which every skilful liar welcomes.

I have no wish to write a brief autobiography: it merely seems necessary to give a few details which, in conjunction with the argument of the book, will explain why I came to Germany at the end of August 1939 to play what humble part I could in working for her victory in the war which I knew to be inevitable.

I was born in New York in 1906. My father's people had lived in Ireland since the Norman Conquest. From my mother I inherited English, Irish, and Scottish blood. Thus, I suppose, the nondescript adjective British could well be applied to my race, though, in fact, I think it is more purely Norman than that of most people who trace their descent with finer feelings.

I went to school in Ireland, where the Jesuits, with whom I had differences, gave me the benefit of their splendid educational system. However recalcitrant I may have proved in some matters, I have good reason to be grateful to them for what they did for me. Nor do I know any better motto in the world than *Ad Majorem Dei Gloriam*.[1]

Later, at the University of London I studied English Language and Literature, History, and Psychology. Much of my study had to be part-

---

[1] "To the greater glory of God"—the official motto of the Jesuits.

time, because my parents had lost what money they had in Ireland, by reason of a devotion to the British Crown—a devotion which seems to have been misplaced and was certainly ill-requited.

From time to time, well-meaning people have sympathized with me concerning my educational deficiencies: but having compared their standards with my own, I feel that their sympathy might have been reserved for more needy cases.

I was brought up by my parents in a creed of fanatical patriotism which the English people found very hard to understand. From my earliest days, I was taught to love England and her Empire. Patriotism was the highest virtue that I knew.

In 1923, I joined the British Fascists,[2] the first Fascist body to be formed in England. In those days, Communism was a lively force in England: and I saw a certain amount of street and hall fighting, of which I shall carry the marks so long as I live. For reasons which need not be given here, the British Fascists, as an organization, came to grief.

Some attempts which I most foolishly made to introduce the doctrine of true Nationalism into the Conservative party met with the ignominious failure that they deserved.

I earned my living as a tutor and was fortunate enough to have a good employer.

In 1933, however, I joined Sir Oswald Mosley's new movement, the British Union of Fascists.

In that movement I became one of the chief speakers and writers: and for three years, I was Sir Oswald's Director of Propaganda.

We had some fine times in that movement—days which I shall never forget. What influence I had I used to promote a thoroughly anti-Jewish policy: and, in this respect I succeeded.

Moreover, I did everything possible to stress the philosophical community of German and British National-Socialism.

To anybody who could see, in the years 1934 and 1935, it was only a specially successful effort to spread National-Socialism widely in England that could avert the tragedy which has come to pass.

Here I should explain that in the course of years and experience the basis of my patriotism had changed. It was no longer the collection of sentimental abstractions that had satisfied me in my youth. Having

---

[2] Formed in 1923 by Rotha Lintorn-Orman in the aftermath of Benito Mussolini's March on Rome, and originally operated under the Italian-sounding name British Fascisti. After suffering numerous splits, the organisation became defunct in 1935 with its founder's death.

seen how the poor lived and how they suffered, I had realized the impossibility of a patriotism which excluded them.

On the one hand, the Tory politicians were ruining the Empire for the sake of international finance: on the other hand, the mere fact that the Conservatives claimed a monopoly of patriotism made millions of the working people detest it.

It became clear to me that it was vain presumption to talk about patriotism until the masses of the people were given some real reason to love their country: and the only real reason conceivable was that a new and scientific economic system should abolish unemployment, poverty, and social injustice.

The more I investigated the facts, the more convinced I became that the old stereotyped patriotism was a hollow sham, designed to conceal the operations of financiers and preserve the privileges of an effete plutocratic caste.

From the outset of my political career, I was always told how unwise it was to mention the Jews. One could condemn the King in public without any fear as to the consequences: but to mention the Jews was sacrilege. For some years I worked to break this evil superstition, and I believe that I succeeded.

In 1937, it unfortunately happened that I had differences with Sir Oswald Mosley on matters pertaining to organization: and I left his movement to found my own, the National Socialist League. In this task I was helped by John Beckett, the former Socialist M. P. for Gateshead and Peckham.

Our little League had a hard and stormy time. In September 1938, I was left in sole charge of it, as John Beckett, though agreeing with me in principle, thought my methods too extreme.

I always held a certain view about the League. There were various movements and societies larger than ours which were, in general, favourable to National-Socialism: but, in my opinion, it was desirable that there should be one which would maintain the purity of the doctrine in the extremest and most uncompromising form.

Moreover, I have always believed, in the face of experienced advice to the contrary, that he who speaks the truth with passion and conviction is a better propagandist than he who burns the midnight oil considering in what way a programme can best be put before the people. There may, of course, be very different opinions on this subject, but as I once said to a colleague who told me that I was damaging my chances in politics: "I am not in politics because I want to get on, but because I feel and believe things that I consider it a duty to utter. Success be damned!" I still think that this attitude is appreciated better than any other by ordinary people.

In the National-Socialist League I came into contact with even more appalling poverty than I had seen in my work for the British Union of Fascists and National-Socialists.

I could give only part of my time to the work. The rest of my time I was earning my living as a tutor with an old friend. As, however, we told all the agencies that we would not take Jewish pupils in any circumstances, largely successful attempts were made to ruin our business.

What seemed most touching to me was the large number of men and women in England who loved or admired National-Socialism but were rendered inarticulate by the lack of cash. Needless to say, cheap stories were circulated to the effect that we were receiving money from Germany.

By this time, Scotland Yard's investigations into the finances of the League should have convinced the Government that nothing could be further from the truth.

Despite my severance from Mosley's movement, I still had many friends in it. I had friends in every movement working for the right cause. Just when it seemed that there were greater prospects of cooperation between those of like mind, the war clouds loomed on the horizon.

Twice in the year preceding the 3rd of September, I was arrested. In all there were two charges of assault and one of an offence under the Public Order Act. I was acquitted on all three and shall always remember the loyalty of my friends who worked for my acquittal.

This was not my first brush with the law. In 1934, I had been tried, together with Mosley and two others, on a charge of Riotous Assembly. We were all acquitted. So far as I am concerned, I can only express the opinion that the King's Judges and the Stipendiary Magistrates are as honourable as the Justices of the Peace are hopelessly incompetent and corrupt. This, however, is just a personal impression, and much depends on how the case is handled by the defendant. I had studied certain aspects of the law to some purpose.

The Police Force of London was very anti-Jewish: but special measures were taken by Sir Samuel Hoare to enforce upon them the dire necessity of pampering the Israelites. Of the hundreds of meetings that I addressed, the Commissioner of Police had notes on every one. I was warned again and again by friendly police officers of some rank to slacken the pace: and I refused. All the circumstances of the last charges brought against me point to the probability that I was arrested at the urgent instance of the Home Office.

We in the League lived National-Socialism. As a small band, we were united in the struggle: and we were all poor enough to know the horrors of freedom in democracy.

One of our members was driven mad by eighteen months of unemployment and starvation. We did what we could to help him: but I am afraid it was little enough.

I lived for months with real friends who loved England and could not get enough to eat from her. Unemployed members who had only two shillings a day came twelve miles by train to attend street corner meetings, or to undertake office duties, spent the surviving pennies on food, and walked home into the small hours of the morning in winter weather. These unknown men were great patriots. They all had the hope that out of their sacrifices a greater England would be born.

So it was with Mosley's men and women too. The misery of these people was indescribable when it seemed to them that all their efforts would be cancelled by war between their country and Germany. They had family ties. Having been brought up as patriots they were benumbed at the thought that there was to be a conflict between their country and all the beliefs that they held dear.

For my part, the decision was easy to make. To me it was clear on the morning of August 25th that the greatest struggle in history was now doomed to take place.

It might have been a very worthy course to stay in England and incessantly work for peace: but I had one traditionally acquired or inherited prejudice, which many will think foolish and which may be logically difficult to defend.

England was going to war. I felt that if for perfect reasons of conscience, I could not fight for her, I must give her up for ever. Such an argument I do not commend to anybody else: but man is guided by more than reason alone: and in this great conflict, I wanted to play a clear and definite part.

In small matters, it is easy enough to be guided by conventional loyalty.

In great matters, a man has the right to hold himself responsible to Higher Justice alone.

Apart from my absolute belief in National-Socialism and my conviction of Hitler's superhuman heroism, I had always been attracted to Germany.

Perhaps the attraction was due to the German blood which flowed in the veins of some of my ancestors: it was no doubt helped by my veneration for the genius of men like Wagner and Goethe. Perchance my studies in Germanic Philology did much to make me aware of racial bonds that time and money have obscured.

Whatever the reason may be, I grew up with that mystical attraction which has ended by my making Germany my permanent home.

My hopes of being able to play some part of a definite kind, however small, in this struggle have been realized, thanks to the wonderful kindness and trust with which I, as a stranger, was greeted.

It would be impossible for me to close this preface without adding that my wife has been of inestimable help to me. It was through National-Socialism that we met: and it was therefore only fitting that our decision to leave London for Germany on August 25th, 1939, was a joint decision.

It was no small sacrifice for her to pack a few things into some suitcases and leave without even being able to say farewell to her parents: but the sacred purpose of this struggle to free the world offers more than ample compensation for any human sacrifice.

Finally, I should like to add that this book is in no sense an official publication. In no way are the authorities of the Reich to be held responsible for any opinion which I may express.

That I have been permitted to write freely what I would is due to that respect for freedom of honest expression which I have found everywhere in Germany since my arrival. Certainly propaganda against the state and people is not permitted: but, with this natural reservation, I can say that the authorities here display a breadth of mind which, to anybody who has read the English press, must seem astonishing.

The ideological reasons which have caused me to place my entire services at the disposal of the Third Reich are stated in the following chapters.

Chapter I: Historical Background

HOW much can be learnt from history has long been a matter of speculation. Much depends on the capacity of the pupil.

There is probably no branch of learning, except economics, in which conjecture plays so large a part. Almost any set of facts can be selected, in a partial fashion, to prove any theory, however, absurd. In this chapter, no attempt will be made at philosophical generalization.

Our only purpose is to show how England's historical development contributed to the fateful and fatal action which her Government took on September 3rd, 1939.[3]

There is a certain dramatic irony in Mr. Chamberlain's[4] choice of the date. For September 3rd was the date of Oliver Cromwell's birth and also of his death. And how much the England of today owes to Cromwell is appreciated by very few. That crude, tough, ugly, self-righteous figure still has its admirers.

Even scholars so discerning and so essentially honest as Thomas Carlyle[5] have paid tribute to it. And most of the English Liberals, who eschew dictatorship, have worshipped at the shrine of this military autocrat because he was the first Englishman to achieve a complete metaphysical unity between Bible, cash, and sword.

---

[3] The date of Britain's declaration of war against Germany.

[4] Arthur Neville Chamberlain (1869–1940), a Conservative politician who served as Prime Minister of the United Kingdom from May 1937 to May 1940. He resigned on May 10, 1940, after the Allies were forced to retreat from Norway, as he believed a government supported by all parties was essential, and the Labour and Liberal parties would not join a government headed by him. He was succeeded by Winston Churchill. Before ill health forced him to resign he was an important member of Churchill's War Cabinet, heading it in the new premier's absence. Chamberlain died of cancer six months after leaving the premiership.

[5] Thomas Carlyle (1795–1881) was a Scottish philosopher, satirical writer, essayist, historian and teacher. Considered one of the most important social commentators of his time, he presented many lectures during his lifetime with certain acclaim in the Victorian era. One of those conferences resulted in his famous work *On Heroes, Hero-Worship, and The Heroic in History* where he explains that the key role in history lies in the actions of the "Great Man", claiming that "History is nothing but the biography of the Great Man".

The reader must not think that we are intent on arguing the virtues of Charles I, the good father and the faithful husband. On the contrary, if this prosaically pious person had known how to keep his word, if he had not regarded himself as the Almighty's Ambassador to England, it is quite possible that the name of Oliver Cromwell would have remained shrouded in the mediocrity from which it emerged.

Fate decreed otherwise. In 1642 there broke out the English Civil War, destined to involve the whole of the British Isles in strife. On the one side was Charles representing unlimited monarchy, the Church of England, and, in some small measure, a feudal concept of society; on the other side was a very odd combination indeed.

It was essentially a party welded together out of the merchant and Puritan factions which already in the days of Queen Elizabeth had shown signs of truculence. The Tudor despotism had been established in 1485 because trade would have been impossible without firm government and also because the whole country was sick of perennial brawling amongst the remnants of the old aristocracy.

No sooner, however, had this autocracy, this dictatorship, brought prosperity to the English people than a movement started to depose it. Nothing in the world could be more natural than that the merchant princes, fattened with the spoils of the New World, should object to paying taxes—and heavy taxes at that—to the throne from which their success had been derived.

So early in English history did there appear the sinister tendency to regard money and power as synonymous. Now this new plutocracy was enthusiastically supported by the Puritans.

These earnest, if fanatical, extremists had undoubted grievances. They were certainly forbidden to practise their religion. They were, in many cases, persecuted with the intolerance of the age, just as were the Roman Catholics.

These Puritans, however, had drunk all too deeply of Jewish philosophy. They were not content to read the Old Testament. They must needs identify themselves with the figures in it. They called themselves by such names as "Hew-Agag-In-Pieces-Before-The-Lord". Ben Jonson was hardly exaggerating when he called his Puritans *Tribulation Wholesome* and *Zeal-in-Me-Land*.[6]

Certainly the materialism of the Jews, as exposed in the Old Testament, had bitten deeply into their souls: for with all their psalms

---

[6] From Jonson's five-act play, *Bartholomew Fayre: A Comedy,* first staged in 1614.

and all their hymns, they soon began to make money hand over fist. By some rather obscure process, they gradually insinuated themselves into the merchant classes, perhaps because their religion allowed them no vice except that of loving money. If their entry into the plutocracy is not easy to explain, there is no difficulty in explaining why so many merchants became Puritans.

The reason was that it sounded much more dignified to protest against the Crown in defence of religious liberty than in attempted evasion of taxes. Thus, under the pretext of fighting for pure Protestantism, many wealthy personages waged a great battle for political supremacy.

The Cavaliers had some idea of the truth: but they were very far from trusting their Royal Leader. The fate of Strafford[7] had shown just how much personal loyalty was to be expected from Charles.

The King's cause was supported by at least half the population of England: but a trustworthy leadership was lacking, and Parliament had the money of the City of London. The Royalists had no more than what they could raise on their estates and their family plate. It was truly a war between Mammon and the Legions of the Lost.[8]

Mammon won. Cromwell emerged as the military dictator of the revolution. Not only did he execute the King, but he gave the Parliamentary babblers short shrift as well.

If the war had been fought in defence of Parliamentary liberty, the leader of the Parliamentary forces showed no hesitation in having literally kicked out of Parliament any members who disagreed with him.

One freak assembly after another was set up by this remarkable man in a pathetically ineffectual attempt to prove that he believed in popular representation: but his real intentions were never revealed until he placed the whole country under the administration of ten Major-Generals, who were mainly concerned with preventing people from eating mince pies at Christmas or playing games on Sunday.

---

[7] Thomas Wentworth, 1st Earl of Strafford (1593 –1641). He served in Parliament and was a supporter of King Charles I. From 1632–39 he was Lord Deputy of Ireland, where he established a strong authoritarian rule. Recalled to England, he became a leading advisor to the king, attempting to strengthen the royal position against Parliament. When Parliament condemned him to death, Charles signed the death warrant and Wentworth was executed.

[8] From the poetic work *Paradise Lost* by the English poet John Milton (1608–1674). Mammon, in the New Testament of the Bible, is material wealth or greed, most often personified as a deity. The lost legions come from Milton's lines; "That all these puissant Legions, whose exile hath emptied Heaven…"

One memorable positive act must be written down to Cromwell's account. He readmitted the Jews to England, whence they had been banished many centuries before by that eminently wise monarch, Edward I.[9]

It is more than probable that the Jewish moneylenders had helped the City of London to gain its victory over the Crown: and it is interesting to note that after the migration of the Jewish gentry into England, Amsterdam began to lose its importance as a centre of finance. And within 20 years, England went to war with Holland three times.

These are facts: and the reader must be left to draw from them whatever conclusion he pleases.

Holland was, of course, dependent on foreign trade and not on internal sources of wealth: and her decline as a first rate money market dates from the accession to power of Oliver Cromwell.

It is not suggested that these Jewish pedlars of usury brought prosperity to England: but their arrival was the signal for the adoption of that philosophy of commerce which has endured in England even to the present time.

The financial organization of the City began to develop upon certain lines which led to the establishment, in 1694, of the Bank of England as a private money-lending agency to the Government.

Cromwell died in 1658. He had singularly failed to create any constructive system of government. He bequeathed his powers to his humbly incompetent son, Richard, who took the advice of the Army Leaders and retired rapidly into private life.

Within a year, England was in the grip of anarchy. Generals were marching and countermarching, there was no security of property, and once again the wail of the merchants arose: "Give us a Government that will restore law and order and enable us to make money."

In fact, the very class, even many of the same people, who had born arms against their Sovereign Liege, King Charles I, people who had declared monarchy to be an evil thing and an invention of the devil,

---

[9] In 1290, King Edward I (1239–1307), also known as Edward Longshanks, issued an edict expelling all Jews from England. The reason for the expulsion was the Jewish domination of the country's financial system, and their extortionate interest rates on loans. The first major step towards expulsion took place in 1275, with the *Statute of the Jewry* which outlawed all lending at interest and gave Jews fifteen years to readjust. Further tension escalated when it became known that the Talmud specifically permits loans with interest between Jews and non-Jews. The expulsion edict remained in force for the rest of the Middle Ages and was only rescinded when Oliver Cromwell permitted Jews to return to England in 1657, in exchange for financial backing.

now began to clamour for a new King. Sure enough, a King came. The debonair Charles Stuart, who had learnt every secret of sponging and trickery at the French Court, gladly accepted the Throne, firmly resolved never again to set out on his travels. This curious character, by that consummate diplomacy of which he was a master, secured for himself a stronger personal position than any monarch had held in England since the Tudors: indeed, for the last four years of his life, he ruled without a Parliament.

Nevertheless, the principle of absolute monarchy had been dealt a fatal blow: and Charles's power did not survive him. Everything in the character of his successor, James II, was admirably calculated to destroy it.

Meanwhile, however, a revolutionary change had occurred in English politics. The Party System had come into being. In 1679, the words "Whig" and "Tory" became known in every English household.

A great struggle was taking place: and the issue was, nominally at least, whether the Catholic Duke of York should succeed to the Throne. The Tories, or Court party, represented the remnants of the Cavaliers. They stood by monarchy, the Divine Right of Kings, the Church of England, and, to a large extent, the agricultural interest. They were, in the main, either aristocrats or men who believed in a landed aristocracy as the basis of social organization.

The Whigs maintained the supremacy of Parliament, the necessity of Protestantism—the more extreme the better and the interests of City finance as opposed to those of agricultural industry.

They were the successors of the Roundheads, but they had drawn into their ranks a number of people who had no positive convictions but were disgusted with the conduct and character of the Stuarts.

From these indeterminate elements there later sprang such men as Chatham[10] and Burke,[11] to whom no unworthy motives can rightly be attributed. On the other hand, the general tenor of Whig policy was gross materialism, just as that of Toryism was mystical incompetence and a purely negative attitude to the progress which the dynamics of

---

[10] William Pitt, 1st Earl of Chatham PC (1708–1778), politician from the Whig group who led the government of Great Britain twice in the middle of the 18th century. He is called "Pitt," "Chatham," or "William Pitt the Elder" to distinguish from his son, William Pitt the Younger, who also was a prime minister.

[11] Edmund Burke (1729–1797) was an Irish statesman born in Dublin; author, orator, political theorist, and philosopher, who, after moving to England, served for many years in the House of Commons of Great Britain as a member of the Whig party.

civilization demanded. Thus for centuries, England was doomed to be divided, the financial descendants of the Roundheads always making use of the heroic but impractical descendants of the Cavaliers.

It is a very great mistake to believe that the Conservative Party of today represents the old Tory philosophy.

The fact is that after 1745, Whiggery swallowed all that was left of real Toryism: and henceforth, apart from a few forlorn exceptions— always fighting a hopeless rearguard action, the people of England settled down to enjoy or suffer different forms of Whig politics. Thus did the materialism of finance lay hold on England.

It would be tedious to enumerate the various attempts which were made at a resurrection of the Tory Party. Let us agree that it died on the day when the bleak moor of Culloden[12] was strewn with the bodies of those who had thought it possible to restore the Stuart dynasty.

In the meanwhile, the constitution of England had undergone a far-reaching revolution. When, in 1689, William by the Grace of God Prince of Orange landed in England and his father-in-law took to craven flight, a new volume of English history was opened.

William was the man whom the Whigs needed: and many of the Tories accepted him because anything was better than James II. William was a heroic, if sombre, figure. A great fighter, he had the habit of losing battles and winning wars. But his interests were far removed from England. The single object of his life was to save Holland from the scorching splendour of *Le Roi Soleil*.[13] Solely in order to acquire greater resources for his struggle against the French aggressors did he undertake the responsibility of pretending to govern England.

And a man who would pretend to govern was exactly what the City of London wanted. The facade of ancient tradition had to be erected before the crooked structure of international finance that the architects of usury were building for themselves.

William never to his dying day saw into the reality of English politics. The Whigs who had brought him to England treated him as a sort of guest on sufferance; and he was at a loss to understand the interminable intrigues of John Churchill, better known as the Duke of Marlborough, one of Winston Churchill's more presentable ancestors.

---

[12] The Battle of Culloden was fought in 1746 between the Jacobite forces of Charles Edward Stuart against loyalist near Inverness in the Scottish Highlands. It resulted in the final defeat of efforts to restore the House of Stuart to the British throne.

[13] Louis XIV (1638–1715), known as the Sun King (*le Roi-Soleil*), King of France from 1643 until his death.

In his reign, two important developments occurred. First, Parliament, consisting of the remnants of the old aristocracy and, in much greater numbers, the pioneers of the new plutocracy, became supreme. There was nothing democratic in its nature. The vast majority of the people had no votes: but the stage was set for the final struggle between town and country, cash and breeding, corruption and authority.

The second event of importance in William's reign was the founding of the Bank of England. This institution had as its function the provision of money for the Government at a substantial rate of interest. It was prepared to lend from generation unto generation and collect its interest accordingly. The cumulative process has produced mathematically amazing results: for the Bank of England was the main factor in the establishment of the National Debt.

In 1705, Dean Swift[14] threw up his hands in horror and exclaimed: "What! A National Debt of five million pounds. Why, the High Allies will be the ruin of us!" The Dean's propensities for bad language would have had full scope, if he could have visualized the National Debt of thousands of millions of pounds which stares England in the face today.

If only statesmen had been compelled to study the laws of Compound Interest, the fate of the whole human race might have been very different. Even a knowledge of simple interest would have helped in this case. But the gentlemen of the eighteenth century eschewed mathematics which had no application to the card tables. Certain persons who were not gentlemen profited by their simplicity.

Of course, Robert Walpole, the founder of Cabinet Government and first Prime Minister of England knew very well what he was doing. His motto "Let sleeping dogs lie" testifies to the fact that he was concerned with more immediate things and was making no attempt to legislate for those who came after him.

George I, Elector of Hanover, King of England, spoke no English. After trying to conduct business with his Ministers in Latin, he gave up in despair and settled down to what amenities he could find in a land where he never felt at home. He harmed nobody and served the purpose of tradition and the Protestant Succession. Henceforth the King was destined to be a figure-head. Now he could do no wrong, because he could do nothing. George III did try to become the autocrat of the American Colonies. England lost all North America but Canada: and

---

[14] Jonathan Swift (1667–1745), an Anglo-Irish satirist, essayist, political pamphleteer (first for the Whigs, then for the Tories), poet and cleric who became Dean of St Patrick's Cathedral, Dublin.

thereafter the monarchs refrained from any considerable intervention in politics.

Perhaps, by way of exception, we ought to note the headstrong opposition of George III to Pitt's design of giving the Irish Roman Catholics that religious liberty which, if it had been granted in time, might have changed the course of Ireland's history.

Now with the recession of the monarchy into the realms of the obscure, where it pathetically lingers today, party politics began to play a predominant role in English life. Whilst the Whigs ruled England throughout almost the whole of the eighteenth century, they had to contend with opposition: and this opposition was often based on the grounds of ambition rather than policy.

I doubt if anybody can really say what Bolingbroke[15] wanted: but he certainly hated the Whigs.

Long after the old Tories had been buried, a new Tory party sprang up in 1770 under Lord North,[16] this time in support of the House of Hanover. It did not get very far: but it served to provide the prerequisite of Party Politics, namely that there should be more than one party. The more parties, the more opportunities for individuals.

Politics came to be regarded as a lucrative profession, thanks to the system of patronage, whereby gentlemen who knew somebody in authority could secure command of a Regiment in the West Indies for colleagues upon whose wives they had definite if not honourable designs.

As the eighteenth century gradually unfolded itself, two serious conditions began to develop.

The first was the decline not merely of the aristocracy but, little by little, of all values that could not be correlated with pounds, shillings, and pence. Strange it is that a century so prolific in poetry, conversation, belles-lettres, and every form of culture should serve but to herald the drab, remorseless, materialistic industrialism that was already looming impatiently in the offing.

Yet, in the long tale of history, it has ever been so.

---

[15] Henry St John, 1st Viscount Bolingbroke (1678–1751), a politician, government official and political philosopher. He was a leader of the Tories, and in 1715, supported the Jacobite rebellion of 1715 which sought to overthrow King George I. He escaped to France after that project's collapse. Charged with treason, he recanted and was allowed to return to England in 1723.

16 Frederick North, 2nd Earl of Guilford, (1732–1792), who was Prime Minister of Great Britain from 1770 to 1782.

The brilliant Augustan period[17] of Roman literature, in which men of creative intellect scaled heights of achievement hitherto unprecedented in the history of Western Europe, was but the blazing afternoon before the twilight of Constantine and the utter darkness of the centuries that followed him.

The second sinister development was the beginning of that agricultural decline which was destined to continue for nearly two centuries and ultimately leave England in the position of declaring a food blockade on Germany without having any resources of her own.

Charles II, between his bouts of extracting money from Louis XIV and lavishing his undoubted charm on ladies who were only too willing to be overwhelmed by it, devoted a certain amount of earnest attention to physics. None of his entourage could discover why. Neither can the present writer.

Nevertheless, the impetus which he gave to the study of mathematics and natural philosophy had its results. Men like Newton began to formulate laws of science which were to transform the face of the earth. The full fruits of the Renaissance were now ripe for gathering: and the mechanical age was ready to begin.

Sadly enough, however, the new interest in machinery, the new desire to produce goods mechanically, the general gravitation to the towns and away from the country began to produce disastrous effects upon agriculture.

Nobody has expressed this change more poignantly than Goldsmith[18] in the *Deserted Village*.

He writes:
"Ill fares the land to hastening ills a prey,
Where wealth accumulates and men decay.
Princes and lords may flourish or may fade,
A breath can make them, as a breath has made:
But a bold peasantry, their country's pride,
When once destroyed, can never be supplied.
A time there was, ere England's griefs began,
When every rood of ground maintained its man;

---

[17] Augustan literature is the period of Latin literature written during the reign of Augustus (27 BC–AD 14), the first Roman emperor.

[18] Oliver Goldsmith (1728–1774), an Anglo-Irish novelist, playwright and poet, who is best known for his novel *The Vicar of Wakefield* (1766), his pastoral poem *The Deserted Village* (1770), and his plays *The Good-Natur'd Man* (1768) and *She Stoops to Conquer* (1771).

For him light labour spread her wholesome store,
Just gave what life required, but gave no more,
His best companions, innocence and health,
And his best riches, ignorance of wealth.
But times are altered: trade's unfeeling train
Usurp the land and dispossess the swain."

Perhaps Goldsmith is a little inclined to over-emphasize the virtues of poverty: but he wrote with feeling about facts which he knew. In a short work of this kind, it would be impossible to trace all the ramifications and results of the Industrial Revolution: and, in any case this is a subject which will receive some attention in the next chapter.

As a work of reference, I can only recommend G.M. Trevelyan's able treatise on *British History in the Nineteenth Century*. This work, though partial and written from a hopelessly Liberal point of view, gives a very fair picture of the social changes at which I am trying to hint.

In brief, the great migration from the countryside to the towns began. The age of mechanized man was approaching. The new plutocracy and those of the old Whigs who were naturally perverse began their final and terrible offensive against the old country gentlemen.

It was all the more terrible because the old "county families" were not just uprooted and annihilated. They were subjected to numerous mercantile blood transfusions until they had to undergo the final humiliation of accepting Jewish sons-in-law to save the ground to which they pathetically clung.

This chapter is not especially concerned with economics: and we shall therefore defer for a very short time our review of the results which the Industrial Revolution brought to the lives of the ordinary people in England.

The political fact of greatest importance is that the two parties locked in life and death struggle were compelled to call in new allies. The party system had rapidly degenerated into that shameless bargaining for votes which, in one form or another, is the inalienable characteristic of democracy.

In the later eighteenth century, elections were greeted with great joy by the country. For they meant the lavish distribution by the candidates of beer, bacon, and money. Election Agents calmly wrote down in their books: "To the vote of Mr. Ebenezer Smith 30, (thirty pounds)."

Constituencies were most artfully constructed in such a manner as to allow vested interests full play.

At the time of the Great Reform Act of 1832, one M.P. confessed that his borough was an uninhabited house, another said that his was an old mound, and a third smilingly declared that his had been under a pond for the last twenty years. All the same, this system was preferable to that about to be inaugurated.

For the Reform Act of 1832 was simply and solely designed to give the lesser merchants the vote, with the result that the nexus between politics and cash became closer than ever before.

Some 35 years later, the Jew Disraeli[19] decided to bring in the hitherto voteless artisans to counterbalance the petty merchants.

His reward was to be hurled out of office by the people whom he had enfranchised. Even in those days, Jews were not liked by the working people of England.

To summarize, however, it may be said that from 1832 onwards, the whole art of English politics consisted of making promises without any intention of keeping them. And after the enfranchisement of the working classes, this evil principle gained added force.

The Liberal Party, formed out of the scum and dregs of all that was left in the worst elements of the Whig menagerie, posed as the friend of the people, with what justification we shall see in the next chapter.

A new thing, called the Conservative Party, rose in the nineteenth century, representing the pitifully faint effort of the landlords and the more patriotic people to suggest that the state had claims no less than those of the individual.

This forlorn band of idealists wandered along through the drab decades of the nineteenth century, till Benjamin Disraeli found it and quite cleverly led it into the outer courts of the Palace of High Finance.

There it waited until, at the turn of the century, the recreant Liberal, Joe Chamberlain, bought it lock, stock and barrel, leaders, members, and hangers-on. From that time onwards, the Conservative Party was only a more respectable, a more delicate, in fact, a nicer medium for the expression of acquisitive commercialism. Thus, Mr. Churchill in the early days of his ill-starred career, was able, with a clear conscience, to

---

[19] Benjamin Disraeli, 1st Earl of Beaconsfield, (1804–1881), a Conservative politician and writer who twice served as Prime Minister of Britain. He played a central role in the creation of the modern Conservative Party. Born in a Jewish house, he was baptized as an Anglican by his father Isaac after a fall-out with other Jews at their synagogue. Isaac never converted, and remained Jewish, and it is now known that Benjamin's baptism was only a tactical move on the Disraeli family's part to help advance in Christian society.

ask his experienced friends whether he should give, or sell, his services to the Liberal or the Conservative Party. It mattered little which.

If a man were a Methodist and a foreign importer, he would naturally be a Liberal. If a fellow were a soldier, and a member of the Church of England, he would probably be a Conservative.

Both would pay their respects to dividends from foreign investments, and both would probably shudder at the thought of being stopped by a self-contained Empire.

On the whole, the Conservatives were a little cleaner, a little less greedy, than the Liberals.

But they existed only as a sort of foil to the Liberal Policy. Whether in office or not, the poor Conservatives were the perpetual opposition.

The ruthless financiers of the City of London did not wish it to appear that there was only one party in the state. Their aims and activities had to be masked: but, in the end, the Conservatives gained such a following amongst the people that their annexation became necessary.

Joe Chamberlain having performed this feat, the Liberal Party atrophied and died out, until its only living representatives are a few old gentlemen for whom there was no room in the Conservative fold. Its disappearance was made all the easier because, at the turn of the century, there had emerged a new and quite impertinent party called the Labour Party.

These upstarts actually demanded that the workers should have direct representation in Parliament instead of being represented by their employers. Nobody could say what these unreasonable people would ask next: and therefore it was just as well that the Liberal Party should be under sentence of death.

Of course, the leaders of this new movement were mostly common fellows, and a little flattery mixed with bribery in the best of taste would doubtless go a long way. But they actually used such outlandish words as "Socialism", they spoke about the rights of the proletariat, and some of them even used the awful term "revolution".

Clearly it would not do to have two parties as well as this new menace: and accordingly, for some years, although the Liberal Party lingered on, it gradually decayed: and those who would formerly have entered it in search of a fortune, joined the wretched Socialists instead. Not a few succeeded in realizing their personal ambitions.

The essential fact to notice, however, is that from 1832 until the present day, the major technique of British democracy has consistently embodied one principle: "The more you promise the people, the more you may expect to get their votes".

A premium was placed on the making of attractive promises: and the skilful politician was he who could break them and still retain his reputation for honesty. Perhaps there has never been such a master of this ignoble art as Stanley Baldwin.[20]

All the time, the vast masses of the people were living in needless poverty: and the main strategic purpose of the ruling classes was to keep them in contented subjection, the Conservatives by preaching sacrifice and the Liberals, in their day, by distributing pourboires instead of wages.

When the Socialists made their appearance, the paramount necessity was to convert their leaders into honorary members of the ruling classes as quickly as possible; the presence in their ranks of a certain number of young men of "good family" provided both the opportunity and the illusion.

With this general background in view, we can now pass on to a more immediate examination of the economic system which had been gradually developing in England since the beginning of the industrial revolution. We can begin to interpret modern history in the light of the more remote.

If England had lost so much in the period which we have reviewed, she had gained an Empire.

But how she proposed to use it, will not be clear until her economic philosophy has been examined.

---

20 Stanley Baldwin, 1st Earl Baldwin of Bewdley, (1867–1947), a Conservative politician, who dominated the government in his country between the two world wars.

Chapter II: Economic Development

THE reader may have innocently hoped at the close of the last chapter, that the historical discussion had come to an end. In this life, the innocent are often maltreated and the hopeful disappointed.

Our brief general survey was intended to prepare the ground for consideration of those issues which are of major importance today: but no such consideration can properly exclude the subject of England's economic development during the last century: for modern capitalism must be traced to its roots before its nature can be understood.

At the end of the eighteenth century the population of the island was about one fifth of what it is today: and the land was capable of maintaining it. Poverty certainly existed: but it was due to maladministration and to a defective scale of social values, not to any inadequacy of natural wealth.

If England had fewer than ten million people to support today, her economic position would very certainly be different from what it is.

One must try to understand that the Industrial Revolution meant a transvaluation of all values.

People had hitherto been content to live on the land and draw from nature their simple but, in general, adequate needs: with the rise, however, of the great towns, they began to long for the relatively high money payments which, in the first instance, were used to lure the healthy peasant population into the factories.

We should doubtless call these wages ludicrously low: but to the country people they at first seemed high, because they were used to handling very little money and did not appreciate how expensive town life would be.

Having been accustomed to living on food from their own land, they were unable to visualize the snares of urban shopping. It was not, however, the desire to handle more money that was solely responsible for the fateful transmigration that occurred.

Another powerful factor was the destruction of the cottage textile industry by the overwhelming competition of the factories. The genius of men like Crompton[21] and Arkwright[22] had rendered possible a greater, a more rapid, and a more uniform supply of spun and woven goods: but it had, for obvious reasons, put the cottage weaver and spinner out of business.

Thus Goldsmith's *Deserted Village* was not so much a description as a prophecy. Agriculture grew weaker every day: and as the old landlords found themselves in ever increasing difficulties, the Liberal or Whig industrialists determined to make an end not only of their political power but also of their economic existence.

Many years of propaganda were required to prepare the way for the Repeal of the Corn Laws[23] in 1846: but once the Liberals were firmly in the saddle after their victory of 1832, it was only to be expected that the policy of importing cheap foreign food would be adopted, whatever the consequences to the British farmer, who was no longer regarded as the backbone of the country but rather as a sort of pendulous abdomen that kept one warm in the winter but hindered locomotion all the year round.

To understand the passion for Free Trade, characteristic of industrial Liberalism, it must first be appreciated that the employers wanted cheap food for their employees, not in order that the latter might have it in large quantities but for the sole purpose of keeping wages as low as possible.

Indeed, in most factories in the earlier part of the last century, it was a practice to pay either the whole or a part of the wages in kind, chiefly in the form of food. Otherwise, shops were set up in the factories, and the employees received coupons with which they could and must buy the goods obtained by the employer at the lowest prices he could discover.

Anything which tended to raise the price of food meant that he had to pay more in real wages: for it was necessary to keep his workers alive. Any worker who expected more than a bare subsistence was deemed a most dangerous revolutionary and was accused of godlessness or drink, or both.

21 Samuel Crompton (1753–1827), an English inventor, who, building on the work of James Hargreaves and Richard Arkwright, invented the spinning mule, a machine that revolutionized the industry.

[22] Sir Richard Arkwright (1732–1792), an English inventor credited with inventing the spinning frame, and a rotary carding engine that transformed raw cotton into cotton lap.

23 The Corn Laws were tariffs on imported grain designed to keep grain prices high to favor producers in Great Britain.

Anyhow, the greatest emphasis was laid on the desirability of cheap labour. In the end, Parliament was compelled to pass various acts forbidding the payment of workers in kind. Evidence given before a Royal Commission showed that workers used to have to wander into a barber's shop with cans of beer and ask him how much he would drink in return for cutting their hair.

On the other hand, if the rustics were bitterly disappointed with the conditions of industrial life, they were no less appalled by the payment they received than by the length of their working day.

A farmer, of course, is used to long hours, but not in a coal-mine or in a filthy factory of the kind established in the early days. Men were expected to work 16 hours a day: and in the first decade of the nineteenth century, Parliament passed a benevolent act whereby women could not be compelled to work for more than 12 hours a day in a factory.

In some coal-mines, women were used instead of pit ponies. Children from the age of six upwards were forced to work for long hours in these factories and were flogged almost to death if their work appeared to be slack or negligent.

Almost without exception, the employers were good Chapel or Church goers who preached the glories of freedom and democracy, and denounced the country gentlemen as reactionary Tories.

These exploiters of Slave Labour were never tired of mouthing the slogans of the French Revolution about Liberty, Equality, and Fraternity.

As yet, there still lingered the idea that birth and breeding rather than money should prevail in the government of the country. There lingered, also, the idea that agriculture might be saved. These ideas were repugnant to the lords of the new democracy.

The aristocrat, the country landlord, the idealist was represented as the enemy of the workers, who would ever threaten their freedom.

In this atmosphere of God-damned cant there gradually grew up that school of political philosophy which licensed Mr. Chamberlain to say, on the 3rd of September, 1939, that England was declaring war on Germany in defence of liberty.

As there approached, during the last century, the final struggle to eliminate everything that did not reek of materialism, it was only natural that the Liberal Industrialists should found a college of Propaganda. This was the Manchester School of Economics. Tenth rate philosophical hacks were bought and assembled with instructions to invent the science of economics and justify the abominations which the craw-thumping Radical plutocrats were each day practising on the masses of the people. The doctrines of this so-called school were very simple. The great and eternal verity of economics was announced in the golden words: "Buy in the cheapest market and sell in the dearest".

This commandment being devoutly accepted, every other grace necessary to salvation would follow of its own accord. Hallelujah! How Jewish it all sounds.

It followed, of course, that human flesh and blood must also be purchased in the cheapest market and its products sold in the dearest—for the benefit of the dear kindly old employer who erected outside his sweat-shops a tin tabernacle to which his workers must, under pain of dismissal, go every Sunday to thank God they were poor and hear sermons on the blessedness of their simple condition and "station in life".

Then, of course, another grand precept was that of Free Trade. England had a start of almost 50 years ahead of the Continental countries in the matter of this Industrial Revolution. And one of her cardinal misfortunes is that she should have based so many of her calculations on this preliminary and transient advantage.

For half a century she was practically without a rival in the manufacturing industries. Napoleon, despite his attempt to blockade England—an attempt as foolish as the English attempt to blockade Germany today—shaved with Sheffield razors at a couple of guineas a pair, his armies were clad in Yorkshire wool, and many thousands of his troops marched on English leather. It is indeed a matter for wonder that he was permitted to obtain these supplies: but the wonder vanishes when one asks whether the new plutocrats put their profits or their country first. As it is today, so it was then, and so it ever will be, whilst Liberal Capitalism lasts.

Of course, the Napoleonic Wars were a blessing to the English merchants, nicely rounded off as they were by the Rothschild speculation over the battle of Waterloo.[24] "Speculation," I have written, although

---

24 Nathan Mayer, Freiherr von Rothschild (1777–1836), known as Nathan Mayer Rothschild, was one of five sons of the Jewish banking family from Frankfurt am Main who spread out across Europe to establish an interlinked banking dynasty which has survived to the present day. Based in London, Nathan and his four brothers (based in Frankfurt, Paris, Naples and Vienna) established a network of agents across Europe which enabled the Rothschild office in London to receive the news of Wellington's victory at the Battle of Waterloo a day earlier than the British government's official messengers. Taking advantage of the public's selling panic caused by lack of knowledge of the outcome of the battle, Nathan bought up a huge

"swindle" would be a much more appropriate word. Europe was torn and devastated by strife, no European land was safe from invasion, and England, secure in her insular position, defended by her Navy, could proceed apace with the development of her new manufacturing industries, congratulating herself on the fact that almost every nation in the world was glad to receive her exports.

Rosy as this outlook seemed, it had two very grave defects. First, it was regarded as certain that England would for ever remain the workshop of the world: and no illusion could have been more dangerous.

Secondly the vastly increasing prosperity of the few was not reflected in the conditions of the masses. Workers who sought better conditions were regarded as traitors, and even, at times, butchered as at the famous massacre of Peterloo.[25] Still, it suited the Manchester School to chant the everlasting virtues of Free Trade.

At first the theory was that the merchant must ransack the whole world for the cheapest materials he could find, in order that he might make a high profit or at least, through remorseless competition, drive out of the market any rivals, British or otherwise, who might challenge him.

Gradually there crystallized the conception that the prerequisite of good business was cheap labour: and thus the merchant princes of Britain sought the products of slave labour, or at least underpaid labour, wherever it could be discovered; and in the end the glorious democratic principle of Free Trade became synonymous with the oppression of the masses in many countries of the world, in order that the Liberal plutocrats of England might get their materials as cheaply as possible. In these circumstances, there emerged also the doctrine that Free Trade was essential to the policy of international investment.

From what we have already seen of the new plutocracy, we should scarcely suppose that its members would be especially anxious, out of pure patriotism, to invest their money in Britain. Such a concept would savour much too strongly of nationalism. Investment for them was a glorious means of making money, knowing nothing of national

---

number of shares on the London Stock Exchange at greatly depressed prices. Once news of Wellington's victory official broke, the shares rebounded and Nathan made a fortune.

[25] The Peterloo Massacre occurred at St Peter's Field, Manchester, England, on August 16, 1819, when cavalry charged into a crowd of 60,000–80,000 people who had gathered to demand the reform of parliamentary representation. At least fifteen people were killed.

boundaries, national obligations, or national rights. The only rule was: "Invest your money or that of other people wherever, in safety, you can get the highest dividend. Even sacrifice safety if necessary."

Thus arose the school of international finance, in which the Rothschilds and nobility of character was needed: all that was required was a sound appreciation of the laws of profit and loss and the psychology of fools. Such was the path of transition from the hovel to the palace: and such it is in England today.

Only those who have lived in England without money or influence know the utter hopelessness of the system for those who have nothing but physical strength, mental ability, or character to offer. The man who offers his services to the community is spurned outside the Labour Exchange every day: and he is spurned in a thousand other places as well.

Now even in the middle of the last century, there was a reaction to this code of perpetual servitude. Great philosophers like Thomas Carlyle and evil Jews like Karl Marx had much to say on the subject. The Marxian manifesto of 1848 was written in essentially the same language and with fundamentally the same outlook as the treatises written on behalf of Liberal Capitalism.

Marxism was just the obverse of the capitalist coin. The capitalists wanted all private property for themselves. Marx said that there should be none at all. They used religion to cloak the vices of their conduct, and Marx replied by denouncing religion altogether, as the "opium of the people." They demanded unreasonable profits, and Marx invented the cumbrous theory of surplus values as the answer. In his gross materialism, he was completely at one with those whom he attacked. The result of his and other such efforts was the so-called class struggle, a bestial phenomenon exalted to the level of a supreme virtue.

Then, as the merchant princes began to use patriotism as a weapon of propaganda, when it happened to suit their own purposes, the result was to create a reaction amongst the poor in favour of internationalism. This result could not be very displeasing to the disciples of international finance.

Thus international Socialism came into being—a thing as barren, as unimaginative, as grossly materialistic as the evil system which had called for an answer from the workers.

The negative, destructive, soul-destroying doctrines of the French Revolution added fuel to the flames: and soon there was to be seen the pitiful spectacle of a huge working-class being taught by the political Liberals to demand freedom from the remnants of the aristocracy, whilst the other Jewish money-lenders were very able teachers. In fact the mentality of England was developing in such a direction as to enable the Jews to prepare for the blessed day when Britain would be one of their colonies.

These three principles—ruthless competition, free trade at any cost, and the investment of money without any regard to blood, nation, or race are fundamental to the international capitalism in the interests of which Britain has mobilized her forces to destroy National-Socialist Germany. They are the basic axioms of the old order, and they must be kept clearly in mind during the rest of our argument.

Later, it will be possible to elaborate this thesis, when we come to that time at which several generations of money and comfort had converted the descendants of the old plutocrats into imitations of gentlemen; or possibly it was that by force of their wealth they were able to alter the meaning of the word "gentleman", which is regarded with the deepest suspicion in English society today.

Now as the dreary priests of despair intoned the damning law that wages must never rise above the level of mere subsistence, some reaction was bound to occur. So strong indeed was this propaganda and such was the ignorance of the people that a certain monstrous theory gained general acceptance after a while.

This theory was that millions of men and women come into the world to drudge, drudge, and drudge without any moral right to better their positions otherwise than by cleverly parting others from their money.

This horrible notion, still today strongly entrenched in the minds of British capitalists, postulates the idea that the masses of the people must be poor and that they are lucky beyond all their deserts if they succeed in getting enough to keep body and soul together and pass out of the world as poor as they came into it.

Exceptions, of course, would be allowed. If some member of this slave class showed exceptional acumen in slave-driving, if he amassed just enough money to enable him to extract more from somebody else, if he showed a thorough sympathy with the sacred rules, he might find a patron and eventually be adopted into the Order of Mammon. He was said to be a prudent fellow, with a good business brain. Neither physical strength, creative intellect, nor industrial Liberals were

grinding them down with the Iron Law of Wages. No wonder the stupid Conservatives did not know the answer to this riddle! And so the current of English political thought was turned awry for decades and awry it remains today.

Men like Carlyle could speak with the tongues of angels: but once the bitterness of class-war had infected the soul of the nation, hatred began to well up, very slowly at first, more vigorously in this century, and now, at any moment, the gentle welling may turn into a cascade or a torrent that will sweep all before it. Nobody knows, least of all those who made war on Germany.

In the next chapter, an attempt will be made to trace some of the major political consequences of this fratricidal tendency which the Industrial Revolution introduced into English life.

Economically, however, the main tragedy was that nobody saw a way of reconciling private property with a just distribution thereof, nobody saw a way of identifying the individual with the state, nobody was able to perceive the necessity for national as opposed to international investment, nobody could distinguish between profit as the reward of organizing ability and profit as the pirate's booty: last but not least, nobody saw the vital necessity of striking a just balance between agriculture and manufacturing industry.

There was nobody powerful enough to save agriculture from its fate, and what that fate meant to England will yet be written large in the letters of history.

The power of money had conquered and had dimmed the vision of nearly all but those philosophers who warned, like Cassandra, not to be heeded. Slowly and very painfully there emerged a Trade Union Movement, which fought inch by inch to gain a little more money and slightly better conditions for the workers.

It was not, however, until the end of the last century that these Trades Unionists saw that the Liberals who had drugged them with Chartism, democracy, and every kind of ideological soporific were in fact the storm-troops of Capitalism itself. Then they could only form a Socialist Party infected with the same materialistic fallacies as the Liberal Party which they had resolved to discard. All this time, the Conservative Party was bumbling about aimlessly, without any real policy, banging the drum of patriotism, occasionally protesting against the fate of somebody like Gordon, whom the Liberals had betrayed: but of this, more in the next chapter.

Whilst England was thus immersed in internal strife, whilst workers struggled for bread and financiers for supremacy, almost all Englishmen had been hypnotized into the belief that England was the strongest, grandest, freest, and most prosperous country in the world.

The stiff-necked generations of the City were so full of self-righteousness and self-admiration that they failed to see a most fateful revolution that was taking place before their very eyes. Whilst they were still piously filling their coffers, the rest of the world decided that England should no longer have a monopoly in the manufacturing industries. Other nations, who were now living in peace, reasoned that they might just as well produce for themselves, with their own labour and to their own advantage, the goods that they had formerly imported from England. Little by little, England's former customers became her competitors, first in their own territory, then in the international markets, and finally, thanks to Free Trade, on English soil itself. Thus the very basis of England's manufacturing supremacy began to crumble.

Needless to say, it did not break up in a day or in a decade: but the process of disintegration, once begun, continued in increasing measure until, during the last few years, Britain could export only half as much as she imported.

Then, as the crazy edifice of her finance was tottering over its broken foundations, Mr. Chamberlain chose war as the sole method of hiding the facts: for war is a destroyer of values and a great confuser of issues.

Amongst the nations that demanded the right to manufacture their own goods, the German States were prominent. As the three different *Zollvereine*[26] became more closely coordinated, German economic strength grew: and when Bismarck[27] lit his famous cigar on the field of Sadowa,[28] he was also kindling the envy of the Jewish-minded English plutocracy. When, in 1871, the German Empire was proclaimed in Versailles, the god-fearing profiteers of the City of London began to

---

[26] The *Zollverein*, or "German Customs Union" was a coalition of German states formed to manage tariffs and economic policies within their territories. By 1866, the *Zollverein* included most of the German states.

[27] Otto Eduard Leopold, Prince of Bismarck, (1815–1898), known as Otto von Bismarck, was a conservative Prussian statesman who dominated German and European affairs from the 1860s until 1890. In the 1860s he engineered a series of wars that unified the German states (excluding Austria) into a powerful German Empire under Prussian leadership.

[28] The July 1866 Battle of Königgrätz, also known as the Battle of Sadowa, was the decisive battle of the Austro-Prussian War, in which the Kingdom of Prussia defeated the Austrian Empire and became the dominant German state.

suspect that a serious commercial rival had appeared. The influence of Queen Victoria was entirely in favour of friendship between the two countries: and the masses of the two peoples felt a natural and instinctive friendship for each other—a psychological kinship which not even two wars have been able to destroy.

But Queen Victoria's son and heir, Edward, Prince of Wales, began, as soon as he was physically capable, the dissolute life which was destined to make him the royal client of Jewish moneylenders and place the whole of his influence at the disposal of men like Speyer[29] and Cassel.[30]

By reason of the policy of international investment which had now become firmly established, Free Trade maintained its dominion over British commercial policy: but every single day that passed, the major premise on which its theory rested became weakened.

Well before the end of the last century, it should have been easy to foresee that geography and science alike forbade the possibility of England's remaining the workshop of the world.

But greed and clearness of sight do not go together.

Instead of wisely concentrating on her own Empire, England formed the fatal resolve to regard as enemies those who preferred to keep their markets for themselves.

Accordingly, realism was held at bay: and already the Jews had proceeded very far with their conspiracy to enslave the world in the chains of international finance: and no instrument was more suited to their purpose than England.

When Britain acquired shares in the Suez canal, Disraeli naturally went to the Rothschilds for the money. Their rate was higher than that of the Bank of England: but they were already too powerful to have any reason to fear the wrath of the taxpayer. They were so powerful, in fact, as to be the real government of the country.

So Free Trade remained as a holy principle: with the same stubborn rigidity as they had resisted the claims of humanity, the merchant princes refused to adapt themselves to changing circumstances. Confident in

---

[29] Sir Edgar Speyer, (1862–1932), a New York born Jew who became a British subject in 1892 and was chairman of Speyer Brothers, the British branch of the Speyer family's international finance house, and a partner in the German and American branches. He was made a baronet in 1906 and a Privy Counsellor in 1909.

[30] Sir Ernest Joseph Cassel, (1852–1921), a German-born Jewish merchant banker and capitalist whose connections in the banking world allowed him to amass a fortune in mining, infrastructure and heavy industry. One of the wealthiest men of his day, Cassel was a good friend of King Edward VII, prime minister H. H. Asquith and Winston Churchill.

the power of money to buy everything, spiritual and material alike, they believed that they could resist all change: and to this end British foreign policy was directed.

One last feature of English nineteenth century pseudo-Economic Development philosophy requires a few words. That is the conception of the state. In the earlier part of the century, the Manchester School had taught that the less the Government did, the better. This is the classical concept of Liberalism.

John Stuart Mill,[31] Jeremy Bentham,[32] and numerous other quacks asserted that the function of the state was to be a mere watch-dog. Ostensibly the motive of this doctrine was to allow as much freedom as possible to the individual.

Actually the intention was that the Government should not interfere with the methods of the capitalists but should provide a sufficient force to deal with the workers, if they became troublesome. In other words, the plutocrats regarded the state as a police-force designed to protect their private property at home and abroad.

Patriotism consisted in using armed force to defend or extend foreign investments. Meanwhile, the masses of the people were looking in vain to their Governments to rule more vigorously and to regulate social relations in the interests of justice.

Carlyle has expressed the situation in these words: "In these complicated times, with cash payment as the sole nexus between man and man, the Toiling Classes of mankind declare, in their confused but most emphatic way, to the Untoiling, that they will be governed: that they must, under penalty of Chartisms, Thuggeries, Rickburnings, and even blacker things than those . . . Cash payment the sole nexus: and there are so many things which cash will not buy! Cash is a great miracle, yet it has not all power in Heaven, or even on earth."[33]

Thus, with Free Trade, unrestricted competition, international investment, the subservience of the State to business, the materialistic conception of history, hideous poverty, incipient Marxism, decaying

---

[31] John Stuart Mill (1806–1873), a philosopher, political economist and civil servant. He was an influential contributor to social theory, political theory and political economy. Mill's conception of liberty justified the freedom of the individual in opposition to unlimited state control. Most famous for his 1859 work, *On Liberty*, which applied the system of utilitarianism to society and the state.

[32] Jeremy Bentham (1748–1832), a philosopher, jurist, and social reformer who is regarded as the founder of modern utilitarianism.

33 Thomas Carlyle, *Chartism*, Chapter VII: Not Laissez-Faire (1840).

aristocracy and declining agriculture as their retinue, the Four Horsemen of the Apocalypse[34] prepared to ride once more.

---

[34] The Four Horsemen of the Apocalypse are described in the last book of the New Testament of the Bible, called the Book of Revelation of Jesus Christ to Saint John the Evangelist at 6:1-8. The chapter tells of a book or scroll in God's right hand that is sealed with seven seals. The Lamb of God, or Lion of Judah (Jesus Christ), opens the first four of the seven seals, which summons four beings that ride out on white, red, black, and pale horses. Although some interpretations differ, in most accounts, the four riders are seen as symbolizing Conquest, War, Famine, and Death. The Christian apocalyptic vision is that the four horsemen are to set a divine apocalypse upon the world as harbingers of the Last Judgment.

Chapter III: Political Development

AT the end of the last chapter, we had occasion to quote Thomas Carlyle, that great pioneer of National-Socialist philosophy. As this chapter is concerned with the development of the democratic system, upon which he wrote with uncanny prescience, we will quote him again.

A hundred years ago, he wrote: "Parliament will, with whatever effort, have to lift itself out of those deep ruts of do—nothing routine: and learn to say, on all sides, something more edifying than Laissez-faire. If Parliament cannot learn it, what is to become of Parliament? The toiling millions of England ask of their English Parliament first of all, Canst thou govern us or not? Parliament with its privileges is strong: but necessity and the laws of nature are stronger than it.

If Parliament cannot do this thing, Parliament we prophesy will do some other thing and things which, in the strangest and not the happiest way, will forward its being done—not much to the advantage of Parliament probably! Done one way or other the thing must be."[35]

How far Parliament has advanced since that time may be illustrated by a little anecdote from Winston Churchill's book *Thoughts and Adventures*.[36] It runs as follows: "On whether the vote could be recorded before the clock struck four depended the fate of the obnoxious measure. A majority in its favour was assured. In those days it used to take the members of the House of Commons more than a quarter of an hour to walk through the lobbies to record their votes. When the debate came to an end, there were only eighteen minutes left. Lord Hugh loitered in the Lobby. Accompanied by about a score of Tories . . . he literally crawled inch by inch across the matting which led to the portals where the votes were counted. By fifteen seconds the stroke of the clock preceded the end of the division on the measure, upon which months of labour had been consumed by partisans of either view. The Bill was in consequence dead, and the further fortunes of the cause

---

[35] Thomas Carlyle, *Chartism,* Chapter VII: Not Laissez-Faire, (1840).
[36] Winston S. Churchill, *Amid These Storms: Thoughts and Adventures* (New York, Charles Scribner's Sons, 1932).

were relegated to the chances and mischances of another year." Thus does Parliament function.

And what was the "cause", to which Mr. Churchill so solemnly refers? It was simply that of the question whether a man might or might not marry his deceased wife's sister! Upon this topic, then, months of labour had been expended, and the democratic majority was defeated by a trick on the part of a crawling Cecil. This is the system that the British people are now required to defend.

The spirit of Parliamentary Democracy is perhaps nowhere better revealed than in the following report from the *Morning Post* of June 4th, 1937:

"On a point of honour, Old Harrovian" will rally round the Government in the House of Commons today . . . It is the Fourth of June at Eton, and the Government, anticipating a general exodus of Old Etonian members, numbering over 100, have included in their Whip a reminder to this effect, and earnestly requesting non-Etonians to fill the breach. The Whips, I understand, are confident that the Harrow School motto, *Stet Fortuna Domus*,[37] will stand between them and defeat on a division. In party circles last night this had been freely translated `The Government must not be let down.'"

Stet Fortuna Domus might also be translated: "Long live the Stock Exchange!"

Really, however, it does seem tragic that the world should be plunged into the horrors of war in order to defend this parboiled nonsense, especially as Germany had no reason to care how stupidly the British people were governed.

When one studies the speeches of British politicians without knowing anything of England and the conditions which prevail there, one gets the impression that Parliament is in some sense representative of the people. But when it is realized that Eton and Harrow[38] between them have at least 200 members in the House of Commons, some idea can be formed as to how far popular representation goes. To think that the whole business of the House and even the fate of the Government

---

[37] "Let the Fortune of the House Stand."

[38] Eton College, often informally referred to simply as Eton, is an English single-sex boys' independent boarding school located in Eton, Berkshire, near Windsor. It was founded in 1440 by King Henry VI. Harrow School, commonly referred to as "Harrow", is an English independent school for boys situated in the town of Harrow, in north-west London. It was formally founded in 1572 by John Lyon under a Royal Charter of Elizabeth I.

must be rendered subordinate to the buffoonery of Old Etonians who want to assert their social superiority seems fantastic. Yet, such are the facts.

One of the most respected Members of the House of Commons was a gentleman who sat there for twenty-five years without ever making a speech or even asking a question. He did no harm. He made no enemies. He just quietly drew his pay, which, incidentally, he did not need, and died with as little fuss as he had lived. But everybody respected him: because he understood so perfectly how democracy works.

Instances of this kind could be multiplied indefinitely. I remember one day in 1934 talking to Stuart Todd, Member for Kingswinford, whom I had known for some time. He permitted himself the following brilliant observation:

"Our people in the House are getting very rattled by this unemployment business. Some of them are saying that a war is the only way out of it: and, by Jove, I really think they may be right!"

This young man was related, and probably still is, to the Chamberlains on both sides of his family. He was thoroughly competent to express the spirit of the Best Club in the World.

Many volumes could be written on the inanity and absurdity of Parliament within our own memory. Fortunately or otherwise, there is no space here available for this study in moral pathology. Let us, as quickly as possible see how the position in post-war years was reached and then blast sky-high the myth of democracy. The key to this mournful history lies in the subservience to money power of nineteenth century England. Everything that subserved the making of profits was valuable: all that did not was dross.

The poor Conservative Party wandered about from pillar to post, never knowing quite what it was trying to conserve. Men like Hugh Cecil[39] and Arthur Bryant[40] have described Conservatism not as a doctrine, but as a mode of feeling.

They might have added that it is a mode of feeling better than one's imagined social inferiors. This is the secret of the Cockney who votes

[39] Hugh Richard Heathcote Gascoyne-Cecil, 1st Baron Quickswood (1869 –1956), styled Lord Hugh Cecil until 1941, was a British Conservative Party politician and MP for the seat of Greenwich from 1895 to 1906, and then later for Oxford University from 1910 to 1937.

[40] Sir Arthur Wynne Morgan Bryant, (1899–1985) was an English historian, and columnist for the *Illustrated London News*. He moved in high government circles and was the favorite historian of at least three prime ministers: Churchill, Clement Attlee, and Harold Wilson.

Conservative: for there is no Cockney whose condition is so abject that he does not feel better than somebody else.

Of course, where the interests of trade demanded the acquisition of new territory or the retention of old, it was very useful to have a professionally patriotic party which would and gladly would take all the blame for the measures of force involved, whilst the pious Liberal plutocrats sat back and turned up the whites of their eyes in holy horror at the deeds which were being done.

In the English people, there lingered, however concealed, some traces of the Viking strain.

There was an inherent sympathy with the acquisition of new tracts of land: and often, deep down, there lay the feeling that wandering, fighting, encountering danger, killing and being killed were all nearer to the spirit of eternity than the drudgery of a Victorian counting-house desk.

Only when one has experienced the drab and sordid conditions of life in commercial London, only when one has felt the last strain of poetry evading the human grasp, like Creusa,[41] in the relentless monotony of pounds, shillings, and pence, can one understand the latent longing for adventure which, in the popular mind, blessed the transactions of British Imperialism.

The Liberals, of course, could not afford to satisfy this longing. The noblest of their leaders never rose in imagination or outlook above the level of a sedate bank-clerk with singular professional acumen. Their language may have been more exalted.

"Mammon led them on,
Mammon, the least erected Spirit that fell
From Heav'n, for ev'n in Heav'n his looks and thoughts
Were always downward bent, admiring more
The riches of Heav'ns pavement trod'n gold,
Than aught divine or holy else enjoyed
In vision beatific."[42]

The function, then, of Conservatism was to provide just that element of aggressive nationalism which could win empires, whilst the Liberal

---

[41] Creusa was the daughter of King Priam of Troy, as described by Virgil in the *Aeneid*. She was killed trying to flee the city, and her ghost meets up with her hero-husband Aeneas as he searches the city for her. She asks that Aeneas take care of their child and vanishes. Aeneas tries three times to hold her, each time failing to grasp her ghostly presence.

42 From John Milton's *Paradise Lost* (1667).

hypocrites for whom the Empires were being won could intone the glories of universal brotherhood and occasionally sacrifice a General, like Gordon of Khartoum,[43] just to show that they were internationally minded.

These Uriah Heaps,[44] these Victorian Pharisees, whited sepulchres, dead men's bones,[45] talked glibly about the Parliament of Man and the Federation of the World, because their interest lay not in the building of an Empire but in the acquisition of a larger area for their financial depredations.

As good internationalists, they must, of necessity, disavow such an aim: and therefore, they found a most useful weapon in the remnants of the poor old landed gentry who, in their mind's eye, were still winning the campaigns of the Civil War.

Thus, when England's heroes won her battles "in stronds remote",[46] the Liberal Capitalist could wring his hands and say "How horrible!", after providing the money for the campaign.

Truly Loki had the Giants at his mercy.

It must be remembered that the pseudo-nationalism of Parliamentary Conservatism aroused more genuine feelings in the hearts of the people: the instinctive movement towards nationalism was very strong: but neither Liberals, Conservatives, nor people understood the

[43] Major-General Charles George Gordon (1833–1885), was a British soldier who served in the British army in Crimean War, led a Chinese volunteer army in China, and served the Ottoman Empire's rulers of Egypt and the Sudan. He then became the British Governor-General of the Sudan, a post he held until 1880. After an Islamic revolt in the Sudan led by a fanatic called the Mahdi, Gordon was sent back to that nation's capital, Khartoum, with the intention of securing the evacuation of loyal soldiers and civilians. Besieged by the Mahdi's forces, Gordon organized a city-wide defense which lasted nearly a year that gained him the admiration of the British public. The British government refused to become further involved, and only when public pressure to act had become too great, did the government reluctantly send a relief force. It arrived two days after the city had fallen and Gordon had been killed.

[44] Uriah Heep is a fictional character created by Charles Dickens in his novel *David Copperfield*. He is notable for his cloying humility, obsequiousness, and insincerity, making frequent references to his own "'humbleness". His name has become synonymous with being a yes man

[45] "Woe unto you, scribes and Pharisees, hypocrites! for ye are like unto whited sepulchres, which indeed appear beautiful outward, but are within full of dead men's bones, and of all uncleanness."— From the bible's New Testament book of Matthew 23:27.

[46] William Shakespeare, *King Henry IV*, Act I. Scene I. "So shaken as we are, so wan with care, Find we a time for frighted peace to pant, And breathe short-winded accents of new broils To be commenc'd in stronds afar remote."

first principle of true nationalism, namely national unity, which, by definition, must be free from class conflict and class prejudices.

For many years, Liberals and Conservatives vied with each other in making promises to the people. Politics was the profession of vote catching. Consistency had nothing to do with this ignoble calling.

On the subject of consistency, indeed, Mr. Churchill, inventor of the euphemism "Terminological Inexactitude" writes as follows of the ideal statesman (*Thoughts and Adventures*, 1932): "His arguments in each case when contrasted can be shown to be not only very different in character, but contradictory in spirit and opposite in direction: yet his object will throughout have remained the same. His resolves, his wishes, his outlook may have been unchanged: his methods may be verbally irreconcilable. We cannot call this inconsistency. In fact it may be claimed to be the truest consistency."

Probably the object which remains the same is the advancement of his own fortunes.

At the end of his essay, the writer grows tired of trying to prove that the truest form of consistency is the abandonment of principles, and he exclaims "Yet parties are subject to changes and inconsistencies not less glaring than those of individuals. How should it be otherwise in the fierce swirl of Parliamentary conflict and electoral fortune . . . But, anyhow, where is Consistency today?

The greatest Conservative majority any modern Parliament has seen is led by the creator of the Socialist party and dutifully cheers the very Statesman who a few years ago was one of the leaders of a General Strike which he only last year tried to make again legal.

A life-long Free Trader at the Board of Trade has framed and passed amid the loudest plaudits a whole-hearted Protectionist Tariff. The Government which only yesterday took office to keep the pound from falling, is now supported for its exertions to keep it from rising. These astonishing tergiversations could be multiplied: but they suffice."

They do indeed suffice, coming, as they do, from Mr. Churchill's pen. Such a clear picture of the dishonesty of democracy has rarely been painted by one of its most ardent supporters.

The tragedy is, of course, that plain, simple, ordinary people took these politicians at their word again and again, in fact whenever an election was fought. Ordinary Tories believed for years that they were keeping the Empire in being by voting for Baldwin. They looked lovingly on tariffs, were proud of Britain's armaments, hoped that one day something might be done for agriculture, and were glad to be Conservative, because to be so was one step nearer to social distinction. After all, it was easier to shake hands with a baronet in the Conservative Party than anywhere else.

It must here be repeated with emphasis that in post-war years the Liberal parties counted for nothing. In spirit and purpose, the Conservative Party was as Liberal as it could be. The Chamberlains had bought it at the turn of the century: and after the fierce Budget struggle of 1909 and the abolition of the powers of the Lords in 1911, it was a weak and broken thing.

In the Great War it got the protection of Mr. Lloyd George,[47] who found its character more suited to a great appeal for national effort than the Liberal Party, with its tight-lipped parsimony and its pious devotion to profit ever could be.

In the end, there emerged a Liberal animal in a Tory skin: and that was all that remained of the old Party System, except for a few bits and pieces like the Samuels and the Simons, and Winston Churchill, willing to serve under any flag in order to improve their fortunes and minister to their self-admiration.

Lloyd George himself was rejected, in 1922, by the curious thing that he had succeeded in creating. Since then he has been constantly in the wilderness, despising the odds and sods who shared his exile. By the time, however, that the shades of Disraeli and Gladstone[48] had become completely entwined and their ectoplasms had mixed into one homogeneous capitalist dough, a new creation had arrived on the scene—namely the Labour Party.

In the days of its childhood, it represented a simple desire on the part of the working people to get social and economic justice. If its vitality had sprung only from idealists like William Morris[49] or Keir Hardie,[50] it would have grown into a fair or even noble maturity. In

---

[47] David Lloyd George (1863–1945), a Liberal politician who served as Chancellor of the Exchequer (1908–1915), Secretary of State for War (1916), Minister of Munitions (1915–1916), and Prime Minister (1916–1922).

[48] William Ewart Gladstone (1809–1898), a Liberal politician who served as Prime Minister four separate times (1868–74, 1880–85, February–July 1886 and 1892–94), and as Chancellor of the Exchequer four times.

[49] William Morris (1834–1896) was an English textile designer, poet, novelist, translator, and socialist activist whose literary works played a significant role in propagating the early socialist movement in Britain.

50 James Keir Hardie (1856–1915), a Scottish socialist and labour leader. Elected as the first independent Labour Member of Parliament to the British Parliament, he was

early life, however, its endocrine glands were poisoned by Liberal politics, Marxist materialism, and the crazy doctrines of Rousseau[51] and the French Revolution. Thus it grew up into a monstrosity, well matched, indeed, with the Liberal body in the Tory skin.

Between these two Blatant Beasts,[52] the English people had to choose. One stood for reform and internationalist nonsense: the other stood for capitalism and what it called patriotism. The greatest tragedy of all was that the more the capitalists wagged the Union Jack, the more the Labour men got to hate it, until they finally fell into the grave error of regarding nationalism and capitalism as synonymous.

Exactly the reverse was true. Thus England suffered the greatest ideological disaster that could overcome her. Those who had a splendid case for reform spoilt it by denying their paramount duty to place their own country first.

They failed to see that in opposing tariffs, for example, they were not helping Indian coolies who were being sweated for the purpose of producing cheap goods for the English home market. They wrote and talked all sorts of nonsense about ending the system of private property and failed to attack the international system of money and usury which was really responsible for their grievances.

In final consummation of all their errors, they joined with the Government in September 1939 in the attack on Germany in the name of democracy, thus showing that in the last resort, they were prepared to fight for the Capitalism which they had been elected to oppose. By this time, indeed, they had touched the very nadir of their pathetic career.

In other circumstances, it might have been possible to bring about a fusion of the genuine Socialism and the sincere Nationalism which many millions of the English people felt: such a fusion would have saved the world from war: but it could not be, because neither the nationalists nor the socialists had the requisite leadership.

The Conservatives whom the people thought to be nationalist were chiefly interested in their international investments and the

---

one of the founders of the Independent Labour Party as well as the Labour Party of which it was later a part.

[51] Jean-Jacques Rousseau (1712–1778) was a French philosopher, writer, and composer whose work influenced the course of the French Revolution. His most famous works are *Discourse on Inequality* and *The Social Contract*.

[52] From *The Faerie Queene: The Quelling of the Blatant Beast*, Bk. vi. (1590) by Edmund Spenser.

ramifications of Jewish finance. The men whom the public believed to be the enemies of private property were amassing as much of it as they could for themselves and were in any case either corrupted by the ruling class or else treated with the deference paid in certain parts of the Orient to madmen and rendered politically harmless.

To the latter class belongs Maxton, who was expelled from the Labour Party because he proposed that Socialism should be established within 25 years' time. Such a revolutionary proposal seemed indecent to those members of the Party who had learnt a few fine phrases about "Playing the Game" and the "inevitability of gradualness."

Some of my, readers may not understand how this strange development was possible. A complete answer is found in John Scanlon's masterly *Decline and Fall of the Labour Party*. In brief, there exists in Britain a kind of corruption infinitely more subtle and far more insidious than that for which the United States are famed.

Social patronage is the secret. Take the raw and class-conscious Labour M.P., give him sherry and champagne, surround him with forthcoming Duchesses who laugh at him behind his back, call him by his Christian name, invite him to the country mansion for a few week-ends, give him a few tips for the Stock Exchange and tactfully lend him the money.

If he is able to resist treatment of this kind, and few are, listen to him politely, compliment him on his political genius, his oratory, his encyclopaedic knowledge, and constantly pretend to seek his advice on the basis of give and take.

If that fails, have a quiet talk with some Old School pal in his party and point out that nothing but promotion will have a sobering effect upon him. Promotion usually means having to obey orders. If the work is not yet fully accomplished, try an O.B.E.[53] Above all, try to make him a Mason.

If all these efforts fail, tell him that he is a damned honest fellow and pack him off to Maxton's Mental Clinic, where his bones can rot in peace. Lug him out to a reception once in a while, and point him out to novices as an awful example of what fanaticism and eccentricity can do to a man of brilliant promise who "lacks the touch." Besides, a tame revolutionary in the drawing room is something to amuse the County, when it comes up to Town and has been there long enough to

---

[53] The Most Excellent Order of the British Empire (often shortened informally to "Order of the British Empire") is the most populous order of chivalry in the British and other Commonwealth honors systems.

get bored with the Night Clubs. Also the entertainment of such freaks by the great shows how far tolerance can go in the beautiful system of democracy. Indeed some of those bored ladies who can create no sensation by talking about sexual perversion can often raise an eyebrow by producing some "wild man" who, poor devil, thinks that by taking thought, he can add a cubit to the stature of the working classes.

Behind the corruption of the Labour Party, there was quite naturally a strong Jewish influence. Bernhard Baron,[54] the Hebrew proprietor of Carreras Tobacco Company, financed the Labour Party very heavily indeed, only of course for the sake of gaining influence in its councils.

In the summer of 1934, when I was Director of Propaganda to the British Union of Fascists, his son, Edward Baron,[55] offered me £300,000 for the movement, on condition that it should not be anti-Semitic. Without even consulting the Leader of the organization, I rejected the offer with an impolite message.

This incident is mentioned solely because it comes within my own personal experience. Now, if Mosley's Union, which had not a single representative in Parliament, was worth corrupting, how much more worthy of attention must the Labour Party have been in its heyday!

The Labour Party, moreover, had its uses. It provided some scope for the endeavours of certain Old Public-School Men, like Cripps, Attlee, Marley, and Ponsonby,[56] who found the competition a little too

---

[54] Bernhard Baron (1850–1929) was a Russian-born Jew who immigrated to the United States with his parents as a youth. He invented a cigarette-making machine which he brought to England and sold for £160,000. This cash allowed him to buy the existing tobacco business of Mme. Carrera in 1903. The House of Carreras was originally established in London in the nineteenth century by a nobleman from Spain, Don José Carreras Ferrer. It continued as an independent company until November 1958, when it merged with Rothmans of Pall Mall.

[55] Sir Louis Bernhard Baron, (1876–1934).

56 Sir Richard Stafford Cripps (1889–1952), a Labour politician who served as Ambassador to the Soviet Union and Minister of Aircraft Production during World War II.

Clement Richard Attlee, (1883–1967), a Labour Party politician who served as the Prime Minister of the United Kingdom from 1945 to 1951, and as the Leader of the Labour Party from 1935 to 1955. As leader of that party, he took it into the wartime coalition government formed by Winston Churchill in 1940. Initially serving as Lord Privy Seal, he was appointed Deputy Prime Minister two years later.

James Marley (1893–1954), a Labour politician who was twice elected to Parliament December 1923 and October 1924 and between May 1929 and October 1931. An early proponent of racial equality, he first raised a stir on the matter after black American singer Paul Robeson was refused entry to a London hotel in 1929. Robeson wrote to Marley complaining about his treatment and the letter was made public, causing an

close in the Conservative Party. In the last Labour administration, the Cabinet contained nine delegates from Eton; Harrow, and Winchester: and there was also room for a few people of "humble birth," who had learnt how to "play the game."

Just as a generation before Winston Churchill metaphorically tossed up the coin to decide which of the parties should be favoured with his presence, so in recent years the young plutocrat on the threshold of politics gave at least his consideration to the idea of joining the Socialist party. Quite a few of the tag-ends of decadent aristocracy showed the same condescension.

Thus, whilst the ruling classes laughed up their sleeves at the Socialists, deluded workmen sang the Red Flag, Communism gained some adherents, and the Jewish organizers of the extreme Left armed their sub-human hirelings with razors to attack young Fascists who dared to cry "A plague o' both your houses!"

As early as 1923, a young friend of mine was killed by this scum, dying of blood-poisoning as a result of wounds in the testicles inflicted by a rusty hat-pin. In 1924, an attempt was made to cut my throat: but the razor slashed a quarter of an inch too high. There is something to be said for having a well-fed appearance.

In 1924, Ramsay Mac Donald[57] formed his first Government: and the Court Tailors were visited by the most unusual patrons that they had ever seen. Before the Election, it had been said that if the Socialists came to power, the Stock Exchange would collapse. This threat having failed to deter the electorate, the Stock Exchange went on as merrily

---

uproar on both sides of the Atlantic. The matter led to a debate in Parliament later that year (October 1929) into racial discrimination by English hotels.

Arthur Augustus William Harry Ponsonby, (1871–1946). At the 1906 general election, Ponsonby stood unsuccessfully as Liberal candidate, and was first elected as Member of Parliament in 1908. He opposed the British involvement in the First World War, and was a member of the Union of Democratic Control, which became a prominent anti-war organization in Britain. He was defeated at the 1918 general election, when he stood as an "Independent Democrat." He then joined the Labour Party and returned to the House of Commons at the 1922 general election. In 1924, he was appointed as Parliamentary Under-Secretary of State for Foreign Affairs, and later served as Under-Secretary of State for Dominion Affairs and then as Parliamentary Secretary to the Ministry of Transport in 1929.In May 1940, Ponsonby resigned from the Labour Party, opposing its decision to join the new coalition government of Winston Churchill.

[57] James Ramsay MacDonald (1866–1937), the first Labour Party Prime Minister of the United Kingdom, leading a Labour Government in 1924, a Labour Government from 1929 to 1931, and a National Government from 1931 to 1935.

as before. Mac Donald owed his victory mainly to the inability of the Socialist voters to see that they were injuring themselves by importing cheap foreign goods, the product of slave labour.

For nine months, the Socialists were educated, and then their opponents grew tired of being in opposition, with the result that the Zinoviev letter was produced.[58] It seems to have been found by the *Daily Mail*, Mr. Donald im Thurn, and J.D. Gregory, a high official of the Foreign Office, later dismissed the Service for using his official knowledge to further his financial speculations. Whether it was genuine or not, we cannot discuss here. Mac Donald believed it to be so.

Society said: "Tut, tut! Fancy having things like that in one's possession. Anybody can see that he's not one of us."

So this conceited child of Scotland was hurled into the darkness till he came back to lead a Conservative Government. His education had improved in the meantime.

The Socialists had learnt the difference between office and power. They nearly all felt that they had been ousted from Downing Street by a foul trick: and they were all the more aggrieved because many of them had seen a new life, which they had never before even suspected to exist. It was a pleasant life.

Ramsay Mac Donald almost lived and slept in his Court Dress: and now, to have to put it away was too bad. This brief spell of glory only whetted the appetite for more.

Perhaps there is nothing more pathetic in English history than the corruption of these poor fellows. They advanced upon Whitehall as a horde of wolfish revolutionaries and departed as chastened candidates for the honorary aristocracy. Meanwhile, some very sinister manoeuvres were taking place in the background. Lord Reading, a Jew more happily described as Rufus Isaacs,[59] brilliant lawyer and rascal of the Marconi

---

[58] The "Zinoviev Letter" was a document published by the British press four days before the general election in 1924. It purported to be a directive from the Communist International in Moscow to the Communist Party of Great Britain, and took its name from the apparent signature of the longtime head of the Communist International — and Jew— Grigory Zinoviev (real name Apflebaum). The letter called for intensified communist agitation in Britain. The letter helped the Conservative Party achieve a landslide win in the election which followed, even though the letter's authenticity has always been in question and was denounced as forgery by Zinoviev himself.

[59] Rufus Daniel Isaacs (1860–1935) was the Viceroy of India (1921–25), barrister, jurist and the last member of the official Liberal Party to serve as Foreign Secretary. He was also the first Jew to be Lord Chief Justice of England, and the first British Jew to be raised to a marquessate.

scandal, was plotting a return to the Gold Standard. Churchill, after losing several elections, got into the Government as Chancellor of the Exchequer, and his good understanding with the New York Jews contributed greatly to the restoration of gold as a measure of all values.

There can be no doubt that the Jews of Wall Street pressed heavily for this reactionary measure.

Thus, Churchill, Isaacs, and Baldwin engineered a nefarious deflation with its concomitant restriction of credit. The results, however favourable to certain classes of rentier, were catastrophic for the working people.

The first evil consequences of this monetary policy were seen in the coal fields and the General Strike of 1926 was the answer of the Trades Unions. From the General Strike neither the Socialist Party nor England ever recovered. England lost coal markets which she has not regained.

The Labour Party lost its balance. Its parliamentary leaders had never believed in the General Strike. They knew that the great mass of the people, whatever their sympathy with the miners, regarded it as a false move.

The wiser members of the Labour Party recommended that the Trades Union Congress should merely use its vast funds to enable the miners to hold out for a period longer than the owners could afford: but even now, the Parliamentary Socialists were being accused of treachery by those who still remained workers.

So Ramsay said: "I don't like it, I really don't like it: but I can't see what can be done about it!" and, waving his umbrella, he conducted the singing of the Red Flag at the meeting where the decision was taken and led his men to the slaughter.

In ten days, it was all over: the funds of the Unions had almost vanished, and the leaders of the strike had to admit utter defeat. A last-moment attempt at mediation had failed because Mr. Baldwin was in bed and would not get up to see the Labour delegates. Now he had them in his power.

Sir John Simon arose in the House and announced measures to render General Strikes illegal. These measures were passed triumphantly, and revolutionary international Socialism was laid to rest with full legal honours.

In 1929, Mr. Macdonald and his followers came back to office. People were tired of seeing Baldwin's swinish physiognomy on every hoarding with some such legend as "Safety First" or "Trust Me" inscribed beneath it.

The repercussions of the American crash were being felt in England: and the Socialists produced a new Confession of Faith entitled "Labour and the Nation".

Indeed it was even advanced as the policy of the party. It was not revolutionary: but it succeeded in outbidding the Conservative promises of reform. It won an election.

Not very long afterwards, Philip Snowden,[60] who had become Chancellor of the Exchequer on the strength of these promises admitted in Parliament that he had never read "Labour and the Nation". This is democracy in action.

In 1931, all the traditional doctrines of Socialism were wrung out of the party like water out of a wet rag. As soon as the Cabinet tried to redeem some of its pledges, the City set to work.

Then came the famous flight from the pound. Mac Donald, Snowden, and nearly all the former bright hopes of *Socialism In Our Time*,[61] walked over with bands playing and colours flying into the Capitalist camp.

And the Loon from Lossiemouth[62] was installed as head of a Tory Government amidst the apelike grins of the City Financiers, who regarded this as the best joke of their lives.

As to Ramsay's former army, all that was left of it could be taken to Westminster in a couple of motor-coaches, so crashing had been its defeat in the General Election.

With a great majority, the Conservatives came into power, entrusted by a relieved people to keep the value of the pound as high as possible. In a month, they were deliberately forcing its exchange value to the lowest level attainable with decency, thus, amidst the applause of the multitude doing the very opposite to that which they had promised—doing in fact that thing which, according to their election addresses, must ruin England beyond repair if the Socialists allowed it to happen. Never in history has there been a more heartless hoax.

---

[60] Philip Snowden (1864–1937), first Labour Chancellor of the Exchequer, a position he held in 1924 and again between 1929 and 1931. He broke with Labour policy in 1931 and was expelled from the party.

[61] The 1928 Labour Party (or, as it was then the Independent Labour Party) election program name.

62 A popular nickname for Ramsay Mac Donald. He was born in MacDonald was the town of Lossiemouth, Morayshire, Scotland.

This book is certainly not written from the viewpoint of the Labour Party. It deserved all it got. But anybody who believes that there is either truth, decency, or honour in British democracy would do well to study that little period of English History between June and December in 1931. There were, at any rate, a few honest Socialists, who could only murmur of their leader:

"T'was just for a handful of silver he left us,
just for a ribbon to stick in his coat."[63]

But their protests were vain: and from October 1931 onwards, nobody ever knew and nobody could ever find out what the Socialist policy was or wherein it differed from that of the Conservatives, in itself very nebulous.

The Labour Party provided the useful fiction of a critical opposition: and so fully was this function appreciated that the Government decided to pay the leader of this opposition two thousand pounds a year for pretending to obstruct the conduct of its business.

This delightful arrangement conjures up no picture of the horny-handed, rugged-faced son of the working class struggling with the agents of capitalism and writing in his attic, by candle light, the speeches which are to sound the clarion call of revolution.

Some of my readers will remember how the luckless Jimmy Thomas, who had gone over with the band, was thrown out of the Colonial Office because he was alleged to have spoken too freely about Budget secrets.[64] A very clever gentleman rejoicing in the name of Cosher Bates made use of the information for certain purposes not entirely unconnected with the Stock Exchange.[65] So runs the tale.

---

[63] The first two lines from the 1845 poem *The Lost Leader* by Robert Browning (1812–1889). It berates William Wordsworth for what Browning considered his desertion of the liberal cause.

[64] James Henry "Jimmy" Thomas (1874–1949), a trade unionist and Labour politician elected to Parliament in 1910. He was appointed Secretary of State for the Colonies in the Labour government of 1924. In the second Labour government of 1929, Thomas was made Lord Privy Seal with special responsibility for employment. He became Secretary of State for the Dominions in 1930. While serving as Secretary of State for the Colonies from 1935 until May 1936, he became embroiled in the scandal which forced his resignation from politics. It was revealed that he had been entertained by stock exchange speculators and had dropped heavy hints as to tax changes planned in the budget. For example, while playing golf, he shouted "Tee up!", which was taken as a suggestion that the duties on tea were to rise.

[65] In 1936 Jimmy Thomas was found guilty by a Tribunal of Inquiry of accepting £15,000 from Alfred "Cosher" Bates, which the latter claimed was an advance for a proposed autobiography.

Actually, however, several weeks before this happened, I chanced to see some correspondence, strictly private, of course, between Jew Lord Melchett[66] and Jew Chaim Weizmann,[67] in which it was agreed that Thomas must be removed from office because he was not promoting with sufficient vigour the Zionist cause in Palestine.

Thomas was a kind-hearted old thing, and the persecution of Arabs would not appeal to him in the least. It is only, however, if he chances to read this book that he will ever learn the cause of his undoing.

Here is another interesting aspect of democracy. From the murky history of the past few years, innumerable examples might be selected to show how the people have been fooled by democracy. There is room for two only.

The Labour Party, when in office, introduced that appalling form of inquisition known as the Means Test. Thereby any unemployed person in receipt of public assistance has to undergo a searching examination as to his means. Officials enter his house, take an inventory of his few sticks of furniture, and direct him or his wife to sell any little thing which the Civil Service regards as non-essential to the household.

Relieving Officers who have had to perform this awful task have told me of their disgust at being compelled to inflict such shame and misery on the poor. If this act of oppression were introduced by the self-professed champions of labour, we might well ask what worse fate they could expect at the hands of an openly capitalist government.

The answer is, of course, that the move was initiated by the City, whose pressure the Socialists were too craven to resist. That this heartless method of treating the unemployed should exist in any country is a scandal: but that it should exist in the home of Parliamentary democracy by the consent of both parties is particularly significant.

The second example of democracy as the will of the people is to be found in the circumstances of the abdication of Edward VIII.[68]

---

[66] Henry Ludwig Mond, 2nd Baron Melchett (1898–1949). Chairman of Imperial Chemical Industries, and a director of both Mond Nickel Company and Barclays Bank. He also served twice as a Member of Parliament, the first time as a Liberal from 1923–24, and the second time as Conservative from 1929–1930. An ardent Zionist, he advocated the evacuation of Jews from Germany to Palestine and supported the formation of an independent state of Palestine as part of the British Commonwealth. He was also chairman of the British Agency for Palestine.

[67] Chaim Azriel Weizmann (1874–1952), a Russian Jew who became President of the Zionist Organization and in 1949, the first President of Israel.

[68] Edward VIII (1894–1972) was King of the United Kingdom and the Dominions of the British Empire, and Emperor of India, from 20 January 1936 until his abdication

What sort of person Edward Windsor may be is not material to the argument. The only question at issue is purely constitutional in its nature. It is interesting to see how the sacred constitution and all the principles of popular representation can be scuppered in a few hours at the instigation of a couple of hardened schemers like Baldwin and the Archbishop of Canterbury.[69]

By these two disciples of "unco' guidness"[70] Edward was hustled off the Throne in a week-end. Whether or not abdication should have been forced upon him is a question upon which no unanimity prevails.

Some stoutly affirmed that as Head of the Church of England he could not marry a divorced woman. Unless our recollection is at fault, the founder of this Church was Henry VIII, who had six wives. Of these, he executed two and divorced two in order to remarry.

Edward VII probably had as many mistresses as he could afford to keep, even with the resources of the Jewish moneylenders behind him. Yet History smiles upon these two competitors of Solomon as good-hearted, bluff, cheery fellows.

So much for the hypocrisy of the solemn-faced men who whipped their king out of the land like a cur.

However, we must not be sentimental. The man whose wife was denounced up and down the land by every evil-minded society harridan as an American whore has calmly gone back to England and become a Major-General. This romantic couple whom the ruling classes of England would not touch with a barge-pole in peace-time have been welcomed back in time of war because of their propaganda value, in other words because of their popularity.

There is no question upon which any people has more right to be consulted than the identity of their King or President. At any rate, if the people are deemed to have any rights at all, this right is fundamental to popular sovereignty.

Yet nobody consulted the English people before getting rid of their king. If ever there was a question for an election or a plebiscite, it was this. There was neither.

---

on 11 December 1936. Only months into his reign, he caused a constitutional crisis by proposing marriage to the American socialite Wallis Simpson, who had divorced her first husband and was seeking a divorce from her second. Choosing not to end his relationship with Simpson, Edward abdicated.

[69] The head of the Anglican Church, who in 1936 was William Cosmo Gordon Lang, (1864–1945).

[70] "Unco" is an archaic Scottish adjective meaning unknown; strange, or foreign; unusual, or surprising.

The pompous hardware-monger from Worcester,[71] always trying to ape the ways of a country gentleman, with a canting Puritan whine in his voice, simply pronounced sentence of exile.

Typical was the reaction of that infinitesimal proportion of the population known as Society. Those who had fawned upon the King were the first to turn upon him.

One lady of "good birth" informed me, some weeks before the scandal burst, that Mrs. Simpson was a "very good influence upon the King." She even arranged his carpet-slippers for him.

Next time I spoke to her on the subject, she exclaimed: "That awful woman? Never!"

Hovering about behind the scenes was the Jew, Philip Sassoon,[72] who played the part of Edward's closest confidant until that final night when the white-faced Duke, no longer King, was hurled out of the country under cover of darkness. No doubt this Jew contributed much more to the tragedy than will ever be known.

Meanwhile, a few thousand people who gathered outside Buckingham Palace and sang "God Save the King" in the hope that their monarch would stay were trampled down by the mounted police. Some were arrested and fined for singing the National Anthem in the land of freedom.

Ordinary men and women were stunned: they had no more to do with the decision than the Grand Lama of Tibet, perhaps, in fact, less. When politicians were asked why there should be no election, they replied that it would arouse too much controversy! This was democracy.

Apart from Mrs. Simpson, Edward had committed two great sins. He had encouraged fraternization between the ex-Servicemen of Germany and Britain. Even worse, he had gone down to the coal fields of South Wales and after seeing the horrors which they had to display, he had said: "Something must be done!" This remark was taken as a slight upon the Government.

But something was done, and it was done to him, whilst the people looked on amazed. Compton Mackenzie's book, *The Windsor Tapestry* gives irrefutable documentary evidence of the part played by the coarse and pompous schemer, Stanley Baldwin, who owed to his pipe and his piggish countenance a reputation for honesty, which no single act of

---

[71] A reference to Stanley Baldwin, who was born in Worcestershire, England to a family which owned an iron and steel making business.
[72] Sir Philip Albert Gustave David Sassoon, (1888–1939), a member of the prominent Jewish Sassoon family and Rothschild family.

his career deserved. These events are related not out of any desire to plead the Duke of Windsor's case, but because they give rise to amusing reflections on Government of the people, by the people, and for the people.

According to the theory of the glorious British Constitution, governments and Parliaments are only given mandates by the people at elections to execute some particular policy which have been submitted to them. If new issues of importance arise, the constitutional theory is that the sovereign people should be consulted.

On not one single issue of importance have the people been consulted for a generation. Nobody asked them whether they wanted the Great War. Nobody put before them the real facts of the Treaties of Versailles and asked for their opinion. Nobody asked them whether England should return to the Gold Standard. They were never given a chance to consider the issues involved in the General Strike. Nobody consulted them on Mr. Baldwin's Indian policy.

When a pretence was made of consulting them in 1931, exactly the opposite of their judgement was executed. Over the Abyssinian dispute, England might have gone to war, but the people had no chance to say "Yea" or "Nay."

Then, when the greatest question of the age arose at the beginning of September 1939,[73] no pretence whatever was made of consulting the people. By no conceivable stretch of the imagination could it be claimed that the British Electorate was ever asked to give an opinion on the problems of Austria, Czecho-Slovakia, or Poland.

The decision to attack Germany was arbitrarily taken by a handful of men who were responsible only to the City of London and its Jewish lending houses. No act of despotism could be more complete. Thus, in post-war years at least, the process of government in Britain has been entirely independent of popular judgement and feeling. After addressing thousands of meetings throughout the length and breadth of Britain, I can testify to the fact that there was no general sentiment in favour of war with Germany.

What is so grandiosely described as "Government of the people, by the people, and for the people" is nothing more or less than the exploitation of the people by the politicians for the aims of International and Jewish Finance. If the definition of democracy is "Liberty, Equality, and Fraternity," we must observe that for years millions of people in

---

[73] The declaration of war against Germany which started World War II.

England have not had the liberty to work and eat, that there is no country in the world where class prejudice militates more against "equality", and that the nearest approach to fraternity is a sickly patronage which the higher orders extend to the lower when they wish to make use of them.

Of course, no scientist would suppose that if men were free to develop, they would remain equal, even if they were born so: and likewise, it is obvious that the attempt to make men equal by compulsion disposes at once of freedom: but in examining the arguments for democracy, we have to take the definitions which its exponents provide.

In no sense whatsoever do these definitions fit the facts. The system of government in Britain today deserves one description only: it is a plutocratic oligarchy, materialist in philosophy, Jewish in purpose, and tyrannous in effect.

Chapter IV: Post-War Years in Britain (1918–1939)

READERS who were a little troubled by the denunciation with which the last chapter closed are entitled to ask for some justification of the abuse which has been used.

In order to justify such condemnation, it is necessary to produce facts showing or tending to show that in recent years the Governments of Great Britain have been disgracefully inefficient and criminally at fault in the treatment of British problems.

Indeed, one of the most forceful arguments advanced by Germany in the present war is that the duties of British politicians and statesmen, if there be any British statesmen, lie at home, that no government can have any excuse for meddling in affairs that do not concern it; when it has singularly failed to provide remedies for the urgent grievances of its own people, and that Germans cannot be expected to listen to sermons from English moralists who have nothing behind them but a record of disgrace and failure.

We are therefore going to examine some of the prominent features of British social and economic life in recent years. To survey the whole field would be outside the scope of a library, let alone a chapter: but the examples selected will be fairly chosen.

It is convenient to consider the broad categories of agriculture, heavy industry, the distributing trades, and general poverty in this order. This is not, however, an economic treatise but a social sketch, designed to throw the light of reality on the political situation which prevailed in Britain before the war.

For reasons given earlier, agriculture has long been treated as the Cinderella of British industries. Yet, as present circumstances show very clearly, it was the one vital form of production in which Britain could most profitably have engaged, if she really aimed at playing a part in Europe's affairs.

Agriculture is the backbone of any national existence: for without food man cannot live. Bolts, screws, cotton, and gold cannot be eaten if a good digestion is to be preserved. Yet, the whole economic history of Britain in the last hundred years is one long chronicle of declining agriculture. The premium placed on the cheapness of food was one cause. People were unable to see that cheap food was a poor exchange for the ruin of the nation.

Moreover, the policy of foreign investment had led to the placing of huge sums abroad. As most of the borrowers were unable to pay the interest in gold, they paid it in foodstuffs which they exported to Britain.

These foodstuffs, for reasons connected with lower standards of life on the part of the exporters and faults in the international currency system, cost far less than English food, which became ever dearer as the farmers grew more impoverished.

The recipients of interest did not care. For them foreign dividends meant the opportunity of buying more foreign food and acquiring a stronger lien on what there was in England. In plain language this policy meant that in return for investing his capital abroad, a man gained the right to claim an increasing measure of whatever goods might be in Britain, whatever their origin.

Those who had to pay the price were the workers, whether agricultural or industrial, who found themselves unemployed or their wages depressed, in order that this fat and pampered class might add to its wealth whilst the causes of national starvation were being prepared. It was on these unhealthy foundations that the spurious prosperity of Britain was built.

Thus the whole economic system was designed for the exclusive benefit of a single class: and no question of economics was viewed in the light of the public and general welfare.

For many years, the landowners in the Conservative Party tried to get some measure of protection for agriculture, but their efforts led to nothing but sneers. In fact, ironically enough, they were told that they were selfish to regard their own interests.

Also the masses were frightened with the cry: "Your food will cost you more!"

The masses might have cried: "Then you must pay us more!"

But they were too democratic to be guilty either of such rudeness or such logic. In consequence, agriculture died a lingering death.

For many years, England has imported from abroad considerably more than half the foodstuffs she has consumed. Agricultural experts have declared before the British Association that the land of Britain could be made to yield all the food that its inhabitants require: and they are probably right: for even a casual journey through the country in a railway train is enough to show the careful observer what a monstrous waste of space and opportunity is permitted.

If you wander round the countryside, you will be surprised at the feebleness of the attempt at cultivation: but if you ask the cause, you will be told by any intelligent farmer that it is useless to raise produce, if there are no markets in which it can be sold and that, in any case, he is so tied down by the restrictions of all sorts of boards—bacon, potato, milk and all the rest, that his main job is to keep alive.

When farmers see milk wantonly destroyed, as it has been again and again in recent times, their ideas of economics break down. When they are forbidden by the Government to produce more than a fraction of what they could produce, it is no wonder that they regard agriculture as a matter of low cunning rather than national service.

A remarkable revelation of the whole position has been made by Viscount Lymington, a practical farmer, in his book *Famine in England*. Particularly ominous are those passages written in peace time and dealing with the probable effects of war on Britain's food supplies.

"If one considers," he writes, "the neglected fields and the teeming population of these islands, a starving nation is no fantastic vision but an ever-present possibility . . . If starvation halted armies, goaded men to revolution, and altered maps in the peasant lands of Europe after one war, what can it help but do to Britain, without food for half her people or means to import it? This is what war means to us . . . Lack of food and fuel makes us utterly dependent on others . . . We must not only see why famine must be inevitable in war, we must see the consequences of famine. We rely on imported foodstuffs to the tune of one million pounds a day: it comes over 85,000 miles of trade routes, sometimes in specially constructed refrigerator vessels."

He then goes on to discuss the extreme difficulty, keeping these trade routes open in the event of war. His predictions may have seemed gloomy at the time when they were made: but they have been more than justified by events.

Foreseeing that when imports were stopped, as they have been stopped, a call would be uttered to the farmers to save the country which had so neglected them in peace time, he observes: "The present state of British agriculture is sadly inferior in fertility to 1911. Suffice it to say that in 1914 the old-fashioned type of mixed farming had left great stores of fertility in the soil which enabled home agriculture primarily to save our food position in 1915, '17 and '18. The war exhausted these stocks of fertility and we have never replaced them, so that we are not in a position to do now what we did then. Moreover the better part of a million acres of land has been handed over to the builder and the road-maker, aerodromes, golf courses etc. Another million acres has gone to wilderness, which is called rough grazing or land gone out of cultivation in the official returns. Thus we are not only less able to import easily then in 1914: we are also less able to feed ourselves, and our population has increased."

It is quite ironical justice that one of the most unyielding opponents of protection for agriculture during a whole political career was Mr. Winston Churchill, who, at the time of writing, is First Lord of the Admiralty[74] and who has already demonstrated his incapacity to secure the flow of imports without which Britain must starve.

Before the Governor of a British prison accompanies Mr. Churchill on that last cheerless walk on a cold grey morning just before eight, it is to be hoped that the Chaplain will intone these passages from *Famine in England*, interlarded, of course, with suitable Scriptural texts.

Turning a little from theory to practice, I should like to quote a passage from the *Daily Mail* of December 44th, 1938. It runs: "Farmers in East Yorkshire, one of Britain's great barley growing belts, sent a telegram today to the Prime Minister and the Minister of Agriculture threatening 'open revolt' against the Government unless something is done immediately to help them in their distress . . . The telegram to the Premier read: 'Your Cabinet's decision to deprive great majority of barley growers of the subsidy is inhuman and intolerable. Germany's persecution of the Jews is only equalled by your persecution of the farmers, and your Government's criminal indifference to the plight of farmers is a damning stigma upon it.'"

It is highly improbable that the Yorkshire farmers were in any way competent to discuss Germany's internal affairs: but they were certainly able and entitled to discuss their own.

Of course, their discussion did no good: but it is interesting to note that even then, a body of English producers advised the Government, by implication, to leave Germany's affairs alone and do something to relieve the victims of persecution in Britain.

[74] This book was written in February 1940. Churchill became Prime Minister of Britain on May 10, 1940.

A few days previously, the Minister of Agriculture, Mr. Morrison,[75] was shouted down at Lincoln, where he tried to address a meeting. According to the *Times,* a shout was raised: "1,400,000 (for British barley growers) and £ 10,000,000 for the Czechs! Is that fair?"

These protests show that even in 1938, Englishmen were aware of the dangers which their Government was preparing for them: but as Britain is a democracy, they were allowed complete freedom of speech and not the least attention was paid to what they said.

A Government which has no intention of being bothered by protests or influenced by requests can very often afford to allow freedom of speech. "Thought is free," as Maria says in *Twelfth Night.*

The light in which agriculture is regarded in England cannot be properly understood by those who have not taken some interest in the Tithe disputes in recent years. Originally, each good Christian was supposed to pay one tenth of his yearly produce to the church for the support of his spiritual pastors. When agriculture was the only considerable industry in the land, this payment in kind was just as practical as a money payment.

Early in the nineteenth century a monetary payment was substituted, because the decline in agriculture would have left the spiritual pastors by the Grace of Henry VIII in the difficulty of having to sell their booty on a declining market.

Many of the poor devils were hard up: but, if the State wanted a Church, it should have been maintained either by its own members or by the taxpayers as a whole, according to the point of view.

There was certainly nothing to justify the theory that the farmers should have a monopoly of sanctity and pay the whole lot when their industry had ceased to represent anything like a major part of the nation's wealth.

Moreover, it was always the Bishops and the great wealthy Corporations like Magdalen College that weighed-in most remorselessly to persecute the farmer who could not pay.

It is only five years ago since I saw a farmer's agricultural implements seized and his furniture sold because the desperate plight of agriculture rendered him unable to pay some Bishop or some great College for his ration of Christianity. And then these bleating Bishops have the insolence to declare that Christianity is being persecuted in Germany.

---

75 William Shepherd Morrison (1893–1961), a Conservative Member of Parliament who ended his career as Governor General of Australia.

Certainly their version of the Sermon on the Mount would not be viewed very favourably by the farmers of Germany.

The Government lent the full force of the law to this oppression, despite the fact that only a little while before a Scottish Presbyterian had been gaily appointing bishops to the Church of England, one of them a gentleman who went as near as possible to saying that the Bible was a heap of nonsense. So much for the sincerity which lay behind this persecution.

Of course, when disorder broke out over the countryside, and when it was manifest that many of the farmers could not pay, the Government had to arrange easier terms: but the principle remains. Thus, if a man is a farmer, he has to pay for the maintenance of a Church in which he may not believe. The alternative is to be left without a roof.

The reason for this particular kind of freedom is that England is not only a democracy, but a Christian democracy as well. No doubt if Christ had been a democrat, he would have scourged the poor out of their hovels instead of scourging the moneylenders out of the Temple.

This is not, however, a treatise on religion: and still less is it an attack on any religious beliefs that may linger in England. When, however, a Prince of the Church of England, the Bishop of Durham,[76] talks about "drawing the Sword of the Lord" against Germany to fight for "God's people" (the Jews), one begins to wonder where the border-line between religion and politics may lie.

And one may remember that, a few years ago, the same gentleman was flung into a river by the Durham miners because he had invoked Christianity as an argument against their getting higher wages.

In general, then, the condition of British agriculture is deplorable: and perhaps nowhere is it more pitiable than in the North of Scotland, where the race is gradually being starved out.

In this connection, it is worthy of note that the Scottish fishermen have again and again besought the Government for assistance, and every appeal has been in vain. It is galling for this hardy, independent, industrious race to have to see enormous quantities of fish flung back into the sea, month after month, when they know that millions of British people are undernourished and at the same time to be told that this destruction is undertaken to secure a rise in prices by which they never benefit.

---

[76] Herbert Hensley Henson (1863–1947). An outspoken opponent of National Socialism, Henson repeatedly spoke out against Hitler, Mussolini and Neville Chamberlain's policies.

Whitehall will have itself to thank if the Scottish separatist movement gains ground. After all, those who know the Scots can well be pardoned if they doubt whether Scotland will indefinitely display the patience which seems inherent in the English character.

Every day that the war lasts will exact its penalty from England for having sacrificed the substance of her wealth to the greed of a small but powerful plutocracy.

When we turn to heavy industry, there are several tales of woe to be told. If the object of British policy for a century was to exalt industry at the expense of agriculture, it has not been attained.

On the contrary, the formerly great industries of England are now in a critical condition.

For years, the coal trade has been declining. Even as early as 1911, discontent was so rife in the coal-fields that Mr. Winston Churchill thought it advisable, as Home Secretary, to order the troops to open fire on the miners. Two were killed and many wounded. Even in those days, this great British sailor was preparing to defend democracy.

The strike of 1921, brought about by bad conditions, dealt a serious blow at the export market.

The Strike of 1926 lost markets that have never since been recovered. It would thus appear that the greed of the owners was responsible for the ruin of their industry.

This view, however, can be disputed. It may be said that international competition so functioned that miners in Europe would work for less than British miners and that the latter were therefore bound to be undercut.

At best, this is only an argument against international finance. If the British Empire had been properly organized and used, England should have been able to dispense with foreign markets. At any rate, the Prudential Insurance Company and various other capitalist institutions took shares in the Polish mines and therefore did not have to care whether British miners ate or starved.

They were, in fact, financing the most dangerous competitors that the British coal industry had to fight. The City of London, therefore, had more than merely idealistic reasons for supporting the Polish Government. They knew that if the Polish coal-fields passed into German hands, there would be an end of slave-labour and of excessive profits. This principle applies not merely to coal, but to all heavy industry in which National-Socialist Germany may acquire an interest.

The failing of foreign markets was not the only reason for the distress in the British coal industry. The transfer of naval and other vessels from coal to oil fuel caused a still further decrease in demand.

The home market further suffered through the criminal system of grabbing middlemen who intervene between producer and consumer. Coal sold at the pit-head for 17/6 per ton cost as much in London as 45/- or even 55/- per ton. In general, transport and middle-men's profits have, in recent years, added about 200 per cent to the cost of coal.

Much has been said and written about landowners' royalties: but, in fact, the sum involved in the argument is insignificant in comparison with the factors to which reference has already been made.

Anyhow, if the landowners were to lose their royalties without compensation, they would merely start dismissing their employees. A scheme has been adopted to buy their rights out. It is typical, however, of democracy that it always tinkers with minor symptoms and leaves great causes without treatment.

It should also be noticed that sweeping economies have been effected in the industrial use of coal, with a concomitant decline in consumption. Again, the use of machinery in coal-winning has reduced the potential of employment for so long as a shorter working day may be refused to the miners.

In 1913, 8 per cent of the total yield was cut by machinery, in 1934 as much as 47 per cent. For the above reasons, unemployment in the coal-fields has been damnable. For more than ten years, indeed for fifteen, the average of unemployment in the coal industry has been over 300,000. Whole areas in South Wales and on the Tyneside have been rendered desolate and hopeless.

When Edward Windsor saw the grimy villages of broken down hovels, the men and women haggard with starvation, the children wandering about in rags, he saw what might have been taken for the survivors of a cyclone impregnated with the germs of plague. "Something must be done," he said: and it was done—to him.

Unless the reader has actually travelled for himself in these poverty-stricken areas, he or she can form no conception of what they are like. If some of the smug believers in democracy could take a walk through Cowdenbeith, Merthyr Tydvil, Hetton-le-Hole or Wath, their complacency would be shaken, and they would run shivering to their baths.

When the miner is employed, his average wage is less than two pounds a week. Typical cases are as follows: Two Somerset miners worked for a fortnight and won approximately forty tons of coal. Each man took home slightly more than 23 shillings per week. Two miners in Durham known to me got between them 52 shillings for a full week's work.

Thus the miner gets less in a week than the young sponger about town pays for his bottle of champagne. Indeed his earnings for a month would certainly not keep Mr. Churchill in wine and cigars for a day.

It seems incredible to anybody who has ever given any thought to the matter that this should be regarded as the natural and inevitable order of affairs. If British Governments had had to deal with some races, they would have had revolution long ago: but so much money has been spent on making these poor people believe that they were born into the world to be beasts of burden that revolution does not come easily.

Before men resort to revolution, they must believe that they have some natural rights. In Britain, the tradition of the blessedness of the rich man in his castle and the poor man at his gate dies hard.

We are not here canvassing any theories as to the legitimacy of private property. In our view, private property is an institution as natural to the West as the sunset: but the tragedy is that the many should have so little, not that the few should have so much.

So long as men think that they are born to drudge in the bowels of the earth for 23/- a week without any hope of advance or any wider outlook, it may well be argued that the system of private property does not exist at all except for a small minority. Yet there was a hope for this stricken industry.

Every year Britain imported from abroad an average of 2000 million gallons of fuel oil. The British Association heard an exposition of the oil-from-coal process and approved it. Had this method of producing fuel been adopted, at least 95,000 miners could have been employed at once, as well as 35,000 other workers.

But, said the Government, there was no capital. Sir Thomas Inskip said in the House of Commons that 40 million pounds would be needed to provide a sufficient supply for the Royal Air Force of the fuel that it needed. The money could not be found, he declared. A fortnight later, 40 million pounds were raised in the City, not for the coal industry, but for France. And now England is spending seven million a day on this war. Every form of obstruction and chicanery was employed to prevent this vital process from being developed into a serious industry. The reason is not very mysterious.

Britain had more than 140 million pounds invested in international oil concerns, and the shareholders were drawing approximately ten million pounds a year in dividends. Thus there was certain to be a powerful opposition to the creation at home of an industry which would very considerably reduce the sales of these international companies.

Of course, it was possible that certain of the investors might secure control over such a home industry and make it pay: but it seemed better to cling to the comfortable dividends of established concerns rather than embark upon the arduous and patient work of creating a new industry.

Besides, the transitional period was hound to be a time of anxiety for the rentiers. Thus of the tiny activity in oil production that was allowed to take place, Imperial Chemical Industries, Lord Melchett's concern, had a substantial control, in case it should ever amount to anything.

To prevent it from amounting to anything, however, the Government kindly intervened with a subsidy to which was attached the condition that not more than 4 per cent of Britain's needs in oil should be produced from British coal.

It is doubtful if any more disgraceful story could be told of a deliberate attempt to maim the resources of a nation and prevent them from contributing either to the national defence or the solution of social problems.

The real significance of the conspiracy cannot be understood until it is realized that Jews like Waley-Cohen[77] and Bearsted[78] are each directors of more than 50 international oil companies.

Thus the development of British resources was dependent entirely upon such plans as Jewry had made for the conduct of international finance. A gigantic propaganda was conducted for years to suggest that the oil-from-coal process could never be an economic or even a

---

[77] Sir Robert Waley-Cohen, (1877–1952) negotiated the merger of the Shell Company with the Royal Dutch Oil Company and became a director of the merged company. In 1928, he became chairman of the African & Eastern Trade Corporation, and negotiated a merger with the Niger Company into the United Africa Company.

[78] Marcus Samuel, 1st Viscount Bearsted (1853–1927), an Iraqi-born Jew who was founder of the Shell Transport and Trading Company, which later merged with Royal Dutch Shell. He served as Lord Mayor of London from 1902 to 1903.

scientific success, and this propaganda continued dauntlessly when Germany was showing the whole world how eminently successful this synthetic production could be.

Thus, a typically Jewish greed not only kept the coal-fields idle and the miners unemployed but left England gravely unprepared for the war that Jews themselves were continually urging her to wage against Germany.

The consequences will soon be seen. Not only the Navy but half the merchant fleet is oil-fired. The exigencies of war will require considerably more than the 12,000,000 tons of oil imported annually and once this supply stops, Britain will have to surrender.

Let us turn, for a moment, to another heavy industry, now much lighter than in former years. No short sketch, no summary array of figures, can describe the horrible fate that overtook the Lancashire cotton-belt in the fifteen years prior to Mr. Chamberlain's declaration of war.

At no time in the last ten years have there been fewer than 100,000 cotton spinners unemployed. The real figures are hard to establish, because so many tens of thousands have left Lancashire in despair, so many thousands have passed off the register of unemployment into the numberless ranks of pauperdom, so many thousands have been unemployed for so many years that nobody can trace their fortunes.

There is no space to tell the story of this tragedy. Only a few hints can be given. In the spurious boom after the last war, every device was employed to give the cotton-spinning industry an air of prosperity. In fact, it had done well during the years 1916 to 1922, but not nearly well enough to warrant the amazing transactions that took place.

Financiers wandered round Lancashire, actually going from house to house, urging the poor to sell the pictures off their walls in order to buy cotton shares. This evil advice was taken. The banks, in particular Williams Deacons,[79] advanced as much money as was asked for by those who had security to offer: and 90 per cent of the title deeds of real solid property in the county passed into the vaults of the banks, where they remain today, so that if Lancashire ever did recover, the bankers would take the profits for generations to come.

Meanwhile capital was shamelessly watered: and all the time, England's great engineering firms were equipping India and Japan with cotton-spinning plants which, with the advantage of cheap Oriental

---

[79] Williams Deacon's Bank is now part of the Royal Bank of Scotland.

labour, were bound to bring the mighty looms of Lancashire to a standstill. The more astute leaders of the cotton industry in Lancashire knew what was happening: and they also knew to a day when the crash would come.

As a youngster, I was one day discussing the problem with a relation who controlled a large number of mills and was also a partner in one of the biggest engineering firms in the north of England. I asked him why no real attempt was being made to spin Empire cotton. He replied that the cost of installing the short staple machinery necessary would be high and he added: "It might be all very fine for idealists, you know! I suppose an Imperial system would be the best, if this damned industry were going to last: but, my boy, you take my word for it, this is no time for capital outlay. I'm selling out the whole lot."

He then explained what was happening in the Far East and went on to observe that it was useless to talk about tariffs, because all those who mattered were much too interested in exploiting Oriental labour to let Parliament pass protective legislation. In a few months, he and his knowing friends had sold out: and after them came the deluge.

I shall always remember that conversation. It was so calm and cynical. He was not a bad fellow, although fairly tough. But he just simply said that the situation was beyond his control and proceeded to collect enough to keep his heirs and successors in comfort for a number of generations, whilst other people were getting knighthoods for persuading more fools and more to buy cotton shares. Such is capitalism!

Then came the crash! At first, most people regarded it as the mere result of speculation and watered capital: the banks foreclosed, the mills shut down, and chimneys that had smoked day and night for sixty years belched forth their last.

The fires were drawn for the last time. The yellow skies of Lancashire became mercilessly clear. Soon it was seen that the malady was of no temporary nature.

In a few years' time, Japan had captured 90 per cent of the markets of the Crown Colonies. India, whilst Schuster[80] and Sassoon smiled their approval, had passed a law imposing a 25 per cent duty on English

---

[80] Sir Felix Schuster, (1854–1936), a German born Jew who became a banker and financier in the City of London. He served on the Board of Trade Commission for the Amendment of Company Law, 1905; the Treasury Committee on Irish Land Purchase Finance, 1907–8, was chairman of the Council of the Institute of Bankers, 1908–9, and of the Central Association of Bankers, 1913–15.

cotton manufactures entering the country: and soon, in Lancashire, the textile products of Oriental labour, the work of the sweated coolie, were being sold in the Lancashire shops at prices which seemed ridiculously low. No English worker could compete with Orientals who could live on a few bowls of rice a day.

Now the glory of Free Trade was shown at its very meridian. Whilst Lancashire starved, the Jewish and British shareholders sat back and enjoyed the dividends of slave labour.

Sir Philip Sassoon, a pioneer in the whole adventure, bought more pictures and gave more lavishly exotic entertainments to his friends. In London, all seemed well with England. On the Riviera, all seemed better than ever.

But in Lancashire the gangrene spread, and slow death extended its domain. First the towns like Oldham, Royton, Rochdale, Bury, and Burnley were paralysed. All day long men and women walked up and down the streets to an incessant but silent dead march. They looked at the blue sky and were glad to see the sun again: and then they suddenly remembered that the light of the sun was the twilight of their lives. They wished above all else on earth that the good old yellow pall would descend and swathe them once again.

Then that mighty heart of commercial life, Liverpool, succumbed. Great wharves became derelict, the hum of industry sank into the quiescence of idleness, and the roar of the machines into the small voice of poverty.

When I last saw the proud and forceful Mersey taking its course with unconcerned vigour into the sea beyond, I could not but think of Carthage and Nineveh as I watched the foaming waters charging past the long, shabby, decaying buildings by its banks.

This is the debt that capitalist democracy owes to those who have once loved England. It is the debt owed to a people who were ruined soul and body by the international finance which they are trying to defend today against the principle of eternal life.

If a detailed survey were possible in this book, a dismal story could also be told of the Yorkshire textile industry: but its position has never been so bad as that of the Cotton Trade. If there is any British industry whose condition in recent years calls for ironical comment, it is the shipping trade.

At the time of writing, British losses of mercantile vessels since the beginning of this war total about a million tons. Mr. Churchill, of course professes to regard the situation as highly satisfactory. Comment upon this unending capacity for satisfaction can be deferred to a later chapter, with the assurance that it will be within the power of the German Navy to provide as much satisfaction of this type as the First Sea Lord requires.

It is of interest, however, to note that the British Merchant Marine was in a very poor condition before the war was declared. Indeed, it had for some time been giving cause for the utmost anxiety to those who believed that England's sea-power was inseparable from her existence.

Lord Lymington,[81] for example, wrote in 1938: "It has been pointed out that our grain reserves are less than in 1914. The shipping position is infinitely more serious. British shipping is less by over one million tons than in 1914, but shipping in the British Isles is less by 1,700,000 tons as the Dominion shipping has increased. More serious still is the size of the ships we now have to rely on under our flag. The average ocean tramp now built is 6,000 tons as against 3,000 tons in 1914. Thus we are nearly twice as vulnerable as before, since each ship sunk or disabled means a far heavier loss of carrying capacity."

If these words had been written in recent weeks, they would have been described in England as German propaganda. In fact, they merely constitute an objective statement, the truth of which has been borne out by events.

It is possible, however, to go beyond the restrained language of the writer just quoted and to find in the British Press abundant evidence of the plight into which British shipping had been allowed to sink.

The following passage from the *Daily Mail* of December 8, 1938, shows with what initial disadvantages the British Merchant Navy started at the beginning of this war:

"Since the Great War Britain has destroyed more British shipping than the Germans were ever able to do during the whole of their submarine campaign. By the end of the war we had lost more than one-third of all the shipping with which we began it. By 1921 we had replaced our losses, and by 1930 we had ten per cent more than before

---

[81] Gerard Vernon Wallop, 9th Earl of Portsmouth (1898–1984), a Conservative Member of Parliament from 1929 to 1934. In 1936, he joined an organization called the "English Array." The gathering European war saw him found the British Council Against European Commitments in 1938, with the author of this book, William Joyce. His book, *Famine in England* (1938), from which the quote above was taken, was an agricultural manifesto which included references to the racial overtones of urban immigration.

the war: but now we are well below the pre-war figure. Effective British tonnage available for the carriage of food, raw materials, and troops in the event of war today is only about 14,000,000 tons compared with 17,500,000 tons in 1914 ... Figures given ... by the National Union of Seamen show that the number of British sailors in regular employment has fallen by more than 20,000 since those terrible days from 1914 to 1918. On October 1st last, 232 vessels of 455,667 tonnage were laid up in British ports, compared with 75 vessels of 99,496 tons on the same date in 1937. Japan has captured 80 per cent of our former carrying trade between India and Far Eastern ports."

Facts of this kind play no conspicuous part in the reports which emanate from the Ministry of Information. The *Daily Telegraph* of April 11, 1939, stated:

"The opinion that unless effective Government assistance is given, there will not be a single small coastal vessel on the United Kingdom Register within a comparatively short period of years is expressed in the report of the British Motor and Sailing Ship Owners' Association for the year 1938-1939." The *Daily Express* of May 11, 1939, commented: "When war broke out in 1914, Britain had 3,430 coastal ships. Now there are 904. Then 62,000 men were employed. Today there are 10,000 and many of these have long periods of unemployment in between."

Britannia was once the mistress of the seas. Now she has become a lodging-house keeper for permanent but non-paying Jewish guests. This deterioration in the merchant service was allowed to take place because, once again, cheapness was allowed to dominate the whole scene.

In the early days of this war, Britain was spending seven million pounds a day in a vain attempt to repair the ravages which greed and negligence had caused.

Much of the shipping was in the hands of Jews like Sir John Ellermann.[82] Sir John amassed more than 30 million pounds by the unscrupulous treatment of his employees and the use of every conceivable device to evade the law and the regulations of the Board of Trade. As his millions mounted, his ships got older: but they were

---

[82] Sir John Reeves Ellerman (1862–1933). The author frequently claimed that Ellerman was of Jewish descent, a charge which was just as often denied. However, according to the biography of the poet Hilda Doolitte (better known by her initials H.D.), the lesbian lover of Ellerman's only daughter, Winifred, the Ellerman family was Jewish. (Richard Aldington, Hilda Doolittle, *Richard Aldington and H.D.: Their Lives in Letters,* Volume 4 page 181. Manchester University Press, 2003).

never too old to lose their Insurance Value. It is highly probable that he knew more than any other living man how to extract the maximum of profit from hardly seaworthy vessels: and it is doubtful if any employer in England has ever been more unpopular.

His son,[83] who controls the *Daily Mirror* and the *Sunday Pictorial,* the most pornographic and pornological papers in England, is reputed to "be worth"—as the phrase goes—sixty million pounds. Exactly how this money was accumulated this is not the place to describe: the book might fall into the hands of persons of tender years.

But, at least, we can contrast this huge fortune with the miserable lot of the tens of thousands of British seamen who have been hopelessly tramping the ports of Britain looking for work for many years.

As a matter of fact, more than half the personnel employed in the British Merchant Navy during recent years has been non-British. Foreign seamen would work for less: so the sons of Britain were sacked and, in a great many cases, their places were taken by coloured persons, whose standards of life were very different from theirs but more in keeping with the tastes and traditions of the Ellermans and such like.

Conditions in the Merchant Service were truly shocking: but the men had no remedy. Their Union was powerless. If English or Scottish seamen did not accept the employers' terms, they were told to rot on the dockside.

There was always an abundance of foreign labour "dirt cheap." Thus England lost something more precious than ships. She lost the services of a strong, healthy, traditionally competent body of British seafarers.

She smashed and degraded a profession and the clear-eyed, strong faced sons of the sea became the shambling, slouching, hang-dog faced unemployed, whose spirit was broken through having to go back every day to the wife and kids with the same pitiful story. The Sea will take its revenge.

At this stage, the distributing trades need little mention. Much more can be said when we come to our account of the Jews in Britain: for they hold the key to most of the distributing trades today. It should, however, be mentioned that the 300,000 transport workers engaged on Britain's railways are, in the main, very badly paid.

Despite the vital nature of the function which they perform, they are treated as hewers of wood and drawers of water. Their Unions

---

[83] Sir John Reeves Ellerman, 2nd Baronet (1909–1973) was the only son and heir of his father, and reputedly Britain's richest man. His sister was Winifred. (See note 82).

seem unable to help them, possibly because of the good understanding between their leaders and their employers.

For some mysterious reason, despite the extremely high freight charges, the railways have been doing badly for many years: and it cannot justly be said that the shareholders get fat on their dividends. The road competition of recent years has hit them hard.

The sad state of the railways need not be blamed on private enterprise: for the Government has been constantly interfering without making matters any better. The problem is, perhaps, one of good administration, and therefore unlikely to be solved in democracy.

Shop-assistants have no union and no protection: the smaller shop-keepers are being rushed into the bankruptcy courts by the thousand every year.

The only section of the distributive trade that flourishes is Jewish: and to that we shall come later.

So far, the treatment of industrial decay in this chapter has been conducted in general terms. It is now time to sketch a series of pictures showing in more detail how the breakdown of Liberal Capitalism affected ordinary people. The material is taken at random from the British Press, so that it is not to be regarded as having been supplied from pro-German sources. These little pictures should be studied in particular relation to the individual liberty which is supposed to prevail in Britain and for which Britain is supposed to be fighting. The best way of exposing this myth lies not in academic argument but in an appeal to real life.

The *Sunday Express* of December 4, 1938, reports as follows:

"The Hodgsons live in a basement flat in Pimlico, S.W. They pay no rent: their coal is provided free. But that is all there is to envy about them. Because they enjoy these things for nothing, Mr. Andrew George Hodgson, aged sixty-three, and Elizabeth, his sixty-year-old wife, both almost cripples, have during the past three years been compelled to live on the borderline of starvation. Mr. and Mrs. Hodgson have to keep themselves on 5 s. a week. Officially they are not in want. Rent-free people cannot qualify for the dole or public assistance."

The English reader will have no idea of the disgust and contempt with which the German views this manner of treating the people who have served the community and have become too old to serve it any longer. A reporter, writing in the same issue of the *Sunday Express* relates:

"A short time ago, one wet night, after the open market had finished, I saw an ill-clad, frail old lady picking up bruised fruit, cabbage leaves, and bits of wood. I collected some bits of firewood for her and tied them up for her. She told me she had found a few bones under the butchers' stalls. She would wash them and cook them with the cabbage for Sunday's dinner."

By way of contrast, there can be found on another page of the same journal the following report:

"Money is pouring in from all parts of Britain to help the refugee Jews and Christian non-Aryans from Germany. The Council for German Jewry's Appeal has raised nearly £400,000 in the last few days."

But aged Englishwomen had to pick up offal from the market-place to make the Sunday dinner.

The *News Chronicle* of December 6, 1938, tells this story:

"Frank Bernard Moore, described as an accountant, of no fixed address, told Mr. Walter Hedley, K. C., at Clerkenwell police court yesterday that he had recently been eating food found in litter bins. He appeared on a charge of lodging in the open air and not giving a good account of himself. . . . . Moore: 'I looked in three or four of these litter bins because usually there is some food in them. That is the only way I have been feeding lately.'"

It is doubtful if there has ever been reported a more damning if unintentional satire on the laws of free England than this story of the poor devil who was arrested for "lodging in the open" and failing to "give a good account of himself." The mere fact that the law can produce such asinine phrases is a proof of the remorselessly mean spirit in which it was conceived and must therefore be applied.

We wonder whether Mr. Churchill would like to "lodge in the open" at any rate, even if his food were the contents of garbage bins, he could scarce fail to give a worse account of himself than he habitually furnishes.

The *Daily Express* of December 7, 1938, reports as follows:

"The Prime Minister yesterday rejected the idea of a Royal Commission to inquire into the position of elderly couples who have to live on 10 s. a week, cases in which a man has reached the age of sixty-five, but his wife has not. He said: 'I do not think it would serve any useful purpose.'"

When Mr. Joe Batey, Socialist M.P. for Spennymoor, Durham, who made the suggestion, pointed out that there were 250,000 of such people in England and Wales, Mr. Chamberlain replied: 'The facts are known'. It is this same Chamberlain who is trying to convince the world that he made war on Germany in the sacred cause of freedom.

The sincerity of the humanitarian altruism which he professes can be gathered from the following couple of extracts:

The Times of March 24, 1939, reporting a speech in the House of Commons by Mr. Lees-Smith, states:

"The British Medical Association's figures were that it required nearly 6 s. a head a week to be spent on food by a family in order that a proper standard of nutrition might be obtained. It was found that nearly 30 per cent of the population of the country spent less than 6 s. a head a week on food. That meant that at least 30 per cent of the children suffered in greater or less degree from malnutrition."

The second extract, suggesting that Mr. Chamberlain might have found some grievances to remedy at home, is from the *Catholic Times* of March 17, 1939. It describes an interview with Mr. Williams, headmaster of the elementary school at Blaina, a mining village in Monmouthshire. He said:

"In South Wales a race of pygmies is being bred. The children are growing up stunted in body as in mind . . . The children sit and sneeze during the winter, for they have not enough clothing, and their boots let in water. Every day I come in contact with boys and girls who are on the verge of tuberculosis."

And yet Britain was supposed to be the richest country in the world: the possessor of the proudest empire. According to the scientist, Sir John Orr, in 1936 there as many as thirteen and a half million people in the heart of that empire suffering from malnutrition.

And this is the system that Mr. Chamberlain would force Germany to adopt in the place of National Socialism! Even his age and upbringing cannot excuse his monumental impudence.

Here is another brilliant sketch, this time from the *News Chronicle* of April 15, 1939:

"8 pounds of Meat as Free Meal for 200 children. In one Cardiff centre for necessitous schoolchildren, Board of Education inspectors found that 200 children were having a meal made from only 8 pounds of mincemeat . . . In another centre, declared the inspectors, only one gallon of milk was used to make a pudding for 100 children. Dietary was described as deficient in quality, quantity, and variety. In the school, out of 67 children who were suffering from sub-normal nutrition, only five were receiving free meals. Some of the premises were "ill-lighted, ill-ventilated, and often dirty."

The only authority in a position to remedy these abuses was Mr. Chamberlain's Government, which was too preoccupied in finding new methods of licking Jewish boots to care how many British children contracted tuberculosis.

I now propose to cite a truly remarkable illustration of what British democracy understands by the word "liberty."

The quotation is from the *News Chronicle* of July 18, 1939. It runs as follows:

"Mounted police in rent strike clash! Truncheons drawn! Missiles thrown. Police with drawn truncheons were pelted with stones and other missiles and water was poured on them from the window of one house when rent strikers clashed with the police and bailiffs in Malvern Gardens, Kenton, (Middlesex) yesterday ... Unemployed men—tenants of houses involved in the dispute-.who have been picketing in the neighbourhood for several weeks, quickly mobilized when two 'Black Marias' and two furniture removal vans arrived . . . At the rear of one house, a man was involved in a scuffle with six policemen and two bailiffs. When the man appeared at the front of the house with his face covered with blood, the crowd became infuriated, . . . Miss Alice Flitt, waitress, and John Smith, fish frier, were married at Edgware on July 2nd. Yesterday, a fortnight after their wedding, their home was empty. Even the wedding presents had gone. Showing the reporter his rent book fully paid up, Mr. Smith said: 'We are the victims of a mistake. The bailiffs were able to get into the house because it was empty. They apparently did not know ours was a subtenancy and took our furniture . . . They took our wedding presents as well. We now have only a mattress to sleep on'. Mr. John S. Twiddle, a bailiff . . . who was in charge of the removal of the furniture, said: 'We were not aware that Mr. and Mrs. Smith were subtenants until we entered. There was not sufficient furniture downstairs, in my opinion, to cover the arrears, so we were perfectly in order in taking the furniture upstairs. We knew that it was a separate lot of furniture, but we were within our powers in taking it because tenants have no authority to sub-let. We left mattresses and bedclothes, but we need not have done that . . . We are going to put all the furniture we have removed into the sale room."

Thus spake Mr. Twiddle as the incarnation of English justice. May his name go down in history as that of a humane, liberal, gentleman, typifying the spirit that led Britain to declare war on Germany in the holy name of liberty.

There, in the land of the free, were two people, a man and a woman, who had been married just a fortnight. All that they had, with their poor little income, succeeded in saving was taken away under police escort. Even those little wedding presents, of an emotional and sentimental value not to be expressed in any terms of cash, those treasures extrinsically so cheap, inwardly so priceless, which every woman has the right to keep as the companions of her life up to the time when it comes to an end, even those had to be taken away to sate the demands of democratic justice.

It was not that the Smiths owed anything. They had paid all that was due. But a legal technicality decreed that they should be left with a mattress as the sole relic of the home that they had built up.

Mr. Twiddle was within his rights. He was the worthy representative of the system which Britain seeks to impose on National-Socialist Germany.

And then the clergymen of England, the pompous Cardinals, the bloated Bishops, prostitute the name of Christ from the pulpits where they preach, by their mealy-mouthed claim that this is a Christian war against Germany.

If ever a cortège of Pharisees deserved to be blasted by Almighty God, it is that train of lolling, rolling, over-fed, grimacing, craw-thumping, nasally booming hypocrites who said that the people of Germany had to be freed from Hitler that they might taste the joys of democracy.

It would be possible, if space permitted, to multiply indefinitely the instances of social and economic oppression cited here. Indeed it is pathetic to think that the books of one Public Assistance Officer contain more cases of distress than could be described in several volumes: but such is the fact.

We see, therefore, both in general and in particular, that the British Government had a plethora of problems to solve at home and that the very existence of these problems was incompatible with a system of social justice.

It is perfectly clear that the politicians who permitted their country to be disgraced with such stigmata were in no sense competent to give advice, much less direction, as to how other countries should be ruled: but, the more one reviews the evidence, the more certainly is one impelled to the shocking conclusion that this British Government regarded as manna from Heaven any foreign dispute which might serve to distract attention from the suffering of the British people under the tyranny of democracy.

Grandiloquent phrases concerning the freedom of Czechs or Poles served to drown the whimpering of British children who had not the freedom to eat what health and appetite required.

Sonorous platitudes about the rights of small nations obscured the muttering of unemployed Englishmen who were denied the right to work.

Bombastic and mendacious denunciations of autocracy in Germany kept the British people from realizing that they were the victims of the most despotic plutocracy in the world.

The politicians who represented that plutocracy knew that their system was rotten. They knew that something must happen—and something by no means pleasant for them.

The only way of saving their personal fortunes was to commit everything to the hazards of war, in the hope that Mars might obscure the failure of Mammon.

Chapter V: Finance

IN the last chapter, some account, however sketchy, was given of the deplorable economic condition into which the majority of British men and women had sunk in recent times. It must not be forgotten, however, that there was a rich and contented minority.

Whereas the state of the masses of the people was unworthy of any civilized nation, above all unworthy of a nation which had such resources as England, there was in the land a ruling class which was probably more prosperous than any similar class in the world.

Attached to this sacred caste was an "upper-middle-class" stratum which certainly had no good reason to complain. There were, in fact, two Englands, each ignorant of the other's existence.

If nine or ten people were crowded into a little damp basement in Hoxton Market, there were 550 persons in Britain whose personal wealth had passed the million mark.

The plain fact of the matter is that Jewish Law ruled in England. Those who merely produced wealth were the lowest caste. The path to splendour was the path of exchange. To make the soil yield up a few more turnips was to attract the highly suspicious attention of Government servants. To sit on the fattest rump that good living could provide and wait for foreign dividends to come in was the qualification for national approval and membership of the Order of Sacred Beasts.[84]

The soundest advice that a business-man could give to his son, unless destined for the Guards, would be: "Produce nothing, my boy— not even children. Buy something in the way of shares, if you can, and wait till you find some bloody fool who will pay you more than you gave for them. Also, join the Craft. Above all, do nothing extraordinary. Otherwise people won't trust your judgement."

Now it is the system of international finance that is entirely at the root of all the troubles we have described. But a treatise on finance must be either very long or very short: and this is going to be very short. There is no compromise between the barest outline and the most

---

[84] A reference to the imagery of Freemasonry, and of the lion in particular. Known as the "Lion of the Tribe of Judah," it is one of Freemasonry's most powerful symbols.

exhaustive, and possibly exhausting, thesis. The motto of that Oriental market of Ancient Theories, the London School of Economics, is: *Rerum cognoscere causas* "to know the causes of things." Let us begin, then, with an informative quotation from the good old *News Chronicle,* never-failing source of damning information. In its issue of December 12, 4938, it blandly relates:

"The story of the gold-fixing has often been told. How every week-day at 11 a.m., the representatives of five firms of bullion brokers and one firm of refiners meet at the offices of Messrs. Rothschild (except on Saturday...) and there fix the sterling price of gold. There is, however, a great deal of activity which lies behind this final act—this centralization of the demand for and the supply of gold in one office and the fixing of the price of gold on that basis . . . A price of gold is at first suggested, probably by the representative of Messrs. Rothschild, who also acts for the Bank of England and for the Exchange Equalization Account."

Oy! Oy! Out with the old Equalizer! Really, vulgarity apart, this little description is very rich in unconscious humour.

On Saturday, of course, the crook who has to represent the Bank of England and the Treasury wraps himself up in his prayer-shawl and plays the "*Kol Nidre*"[85] on his sensuous violin, and lusciously meditates on the nature of his operations for the following week.

It is somewhat terrifying to think that this fellow will decide the cost of living, the wages, the prices, and every other economic element in the life of the British people.

The ordinary man does not even know that there is such a person, much less who he is or what he does with himself on a Saturday morning. Indeed, if you were to tell many otherwise well-informed English people that the Jews controlled finance, they would not believe you. The *News Chronicle,* however, is not exactly a Nazi source of information. And, whatever Britain's external relations may be, it is

---

[85] The *Kol Nidre* prayer is still recited in synagogues before the beginning of the evening service on every Yom Kippur, the Day of Atonement. Its name is taken from the opening words, meaning *all vows.* The cantor chants the passage beginning with the words *Kol Nidre* three times, and says the following words (Nusach Ashkenaz): "All vows we are likely to make, all oaths and pledges we are likely to take between this Yom Kippur and the next Yom Kippur, we publicly renounce. Let them all be relinquished and abandoned, null and void, neither firm nor established. Let our vows, pledges and oaths be considered neither vows nor pledges nor oaths." (Translation of Philip Birnbaum, from *High Holiday Prayer Book,* Hebrew Publishing Company, NY, 1951.) This prayer effectively absolves Jews from all promises or pledges made during the coming year.

inevitable under the present system that the control of gold must mean the economic control of British national life: and the Treasury does not even think it worth while to have a representative of its own at this Ritual Murder which takes place every weekday except Saturday at 11 a.m.

To be clear on the whole matter, we must realize that, fundamentally, there can be only two views as to the purpose of money. There may be a thousand intermediate shades of opinion: but, eventually, one is forced back into the position of having to decide whether money exists for man or man for money, whether money is merely a symbol of real wealth enabling commodities and services to be exchanged or whether it is the determinant of all industry by the criterion of which production and distribution must be regulated.

The former is the concept of National-Socialism, the latter is the theory of Liberal Capitalism and International Finance.

Consider the commonest case of commercial absurdity found in Financial Democracy. It is well known that a great mass of people want far more of this world's goods than they have, far more to eat, far more clothes, let us say. But the industrialist does not produce enough.

Ask him why, and he will say: "Because if I do produce any more, the merchant will not pay me."

Go, then, to the merchant and ask him why he does not order more goods. He will say: "Of course I would order them if only I could sell them. Heaven knows, I want a bigger market badly enough."

Then tell him that Mrs. Smith wants more bacon, Mrs. Brown more butter, Mrs. Jones more beef, in fact recite a list of the wants of all those in the neighbourhood, and ask him whether all these people could not constitute a market for him.

He will reply: "My dear sir, do you really think that I am giving my stocks away? Good Lord! People are no use to me unless they have cash." Thus, within a few hundred yards of his stores, there may be thousands of people longing to form the market that he wants. They are willing to work and work hard. The raw materials and the machinery are not lacking. They lack one thing only—the money.

Thus, raw materials, engineering prowess, mechanical efficiency, plentiful labour, organizing ability all count for nothing, because this impertinent factor money intervenes and cries "Halt!"

A market consists merely of people who want to buy and have the money to effect the purchases. This fact, however, is hard to bring home to those who habitually think in terms of money, and that is the vast majority of the English people today.

Of course, the whole object of the system's propaganda is to encourage the population to think in this way. So long as men and women look up to money as the supreme determinant of economic conditions, so long will they be easy to cheat.

So long will they fail to analyse the contents of the gulf between consumption and production.

As soon as industrialism established itself, the majority of people lost touch with the production of the primary necessities of life. A man might make screws, for example, but he could not eat them. Food he must get.

Somewhere or other was a group of persons who determined how many screws went to the pound of bread. Who they were, the worker knew not. Even their locality remained a mystery to the ordinary man. Then, when the pound of bread set out on its travels, everybody who handled it took a slice so that by the time it reached the screw-maker, it had lost a certain amount of weight.

Of course, bakers and carriers had to live: but apart from those honestly engaged in the making and carrying, there was a series of persons called middlemen, whose sole function was to pass the loaf from one to another and take a slice: indeed most of them never saw the loaf at all, but got the slice just the same.

Now the most immoral part of these transactions was not that all these useless people had their whack at the loaf, but that the poor screw-maker never knew and never had any means of knowing what exact relation prevailed between his screws and his bread.

The mystery of this relationship remained in the hands of those who controlled the monetary system or who left it uncontrolled in the knowledge that the pirates and jugglers would make the best of the financial anarchy which went by the name of "individual liberty" and which meant the individual liberty of one man to rob another, if he could do it respectably.

Now these conditions were not limited in duration to the early days of the Industrial Revolution. In England, they reign supreme today. Such, moreover, is the force of the propaganda which international finance can afford to conduct that the supposedly cultured classes in England can see nothing monstrous in the fact that every year enormous quantities of wheat are burnt and great masses of fish flung back into the sea, whilst there are 13½ million undernourished persons on the island.

If you say to them: "This thing is done merely to keep prices high," they will cordially agree and smile their approval, as they think of their foreign dividends. Of course, when a ruling class can sink to this depth of moral perversion, it is not very far from its end.

The notion that the level of production should be controlled by monetary considerations belongs to a very primitive and superstitious stage of social evolution. Indeed, there are few savage tribes that would accept it as it is accepted in Britain today.

Suppose that in some very backward island, a shell standard of money prevailed. Assume also that some malicious or half-witted creature managed to acquire half the shells in the island and to drop them into the water beyond recovery. The chiefs and witch-doctors would have to hold a council of emergency.

But if the rulers of that island decreed that because half the money of the community had been lost, hunting and fishing and tilling must now be reduced by fifty per cent, there'd be a hot time in the old town that night.

In such a simple state of society, the criminal absurdity of the proposal would be obvious to the meanest and most untutored intellect. Yet a policy which the most undeveloped savage tribe would reject as nonsense has been accepted by the British people as a sacred ritual for many years. Thus, of course, international finance, by restricting supplies and causing shortage, can produce whatever conditions of marketing that may be most profitable to itself.

If there is one truth against which the Old School of Finance is fighting today, it is the supreme verity that production of goods should be based on the needs of the people, the only limit being the limit of natural resources and raw materials.

Since the dawn of human history, the great struggle of man has been to wrest from Nature by force and cunning the means of life and enjoyment. It was only when the blessings of modern democracy made their appearance one hundred and fifty years ago, that he was told, in an arbitrary manner, that his efforts must be slackened and regulated henceforth by the private interests of an infinitesimal proportion of the world's population.

Five minutes' honest thought devoted to the whole matter should be enough to clear away the myths, the obscurities, and the mysteries that have been deliberately built up around the system to conceal its inherent wickedness.

National-Socialist Germany realized from the first day of its existence that the main problem of economics was maximal production of the commodities the population required. All questions of distribution must be contingent on the existence of something to distribute, the more the better.

Once an adequate level of production is reached, it is only a matter of totalitarian administration to secure that the money system shall give the people the purchasing instruments whereby they can establish a title to possess and enjoy what they have produced.

Of course, a certain amount of the wealth produced must always be set aside to serve as the basis for further production. Hence the people can never at once consume the whole of what they have produced: but the part that they can consume will be perfectly adequate, so long as the level of production is sufficient and a proper proportion is maintained between capital goods and consumers' goods.

Quite naturally, the operation of a managed currency, whereby purchasing power is equated to the people's needs, must depend upon the absolute power of the state to control all economic elements, including prices, wages, rents, dividends, and profits in the service of the whole people, with no respect to class prejudice.

Such a control is, of course, incompatible with the conditions of democracy: hence the frenzied efforts of the British plutocrats to preserve this democracy, which excludes the only form of organization that could compel the individual to respect the freedom of others as much as he respects his own.

Of course, the moment that Germany revolted against the conception that production should be restricted in the interests of a few High Financiers, she created in the minds of all well-informed democrats the fear that Central Europe would break away altogether from the system of international finance.

That fear was amply justified: but it rendered war between England and Germany inevitable, unless some hundreds of Jews were to swing in timely fashion from the lampposts of Westminster. It would have been cruel to hang them: but the consequences of not doing so will be very much more serious for the world than would a transient act of limited violence. This language may seem strong: but the casualties in this war have already far exceeded the number of persons responsible for causing It. War is both unpleasant and brutal: but the Jewish control of international finance over all these years has been infinitely more brutal than any war could be. To know that one will be shot or blown to bits is distinctly unpleasant: but any man worthy of the name would be far less dismayed by this thought, if he had no dependents, than by the thought that he might be unemployed for years.

If he had dependents, the experience of seeing his wife sinking into tuberculosis and his children growing up with rickets should be much more intolerable than the prospect of a brief agony and a world where democracy is not to be found.

Of course, not one of the men who control capitalist finance today knows how it feels to wait month after month for a job that never comes, to see one's few pence disappearing, and to experience the spiritual hopelessness and the physical illness which come from the thought: "In the whole of this wide world, nobody wants me, nobody wants my brain or my hands. I must go and beg." The well-to-do who read these lines will sneer.

Their derision will receive its ample compensation in the recognition granted by those who have been unemployed in mighty England. Unfortunately, so many of the unemployed do not understand that the arbitrary restriction of production and the control of the monetary system for the benefit of the rich can never mean anything but unemployment.

Lack of purchasing power in the hands of the people means lack of effective demand. Lack of effective demand means less work and more unemployment.

There is another important aspect of the question. One machine today, minded by two men, can do as much work in ten hours as one hundred men could do a few decades ago.

But surely the human race will not wait until ten thousand men can produce its entire needs by the aid of machinery before introducing some reasonable system of labour.

When the stage is reached at which enough and more is being produced by machinery, there will be enough to distribute, and the solution of the unemployment problem will lie in shorter hours.

Whether a man works ten hours a day or five is immaterial so long as maximal production of needed goods is secured. What is vital is that every citizen able to work should be given the chance and thereby earn the ethical right to participate in the distribution. As a matter of fact, although Germany has raised her production in the last few years from 100 per cent in some industries to 2000 per cent in others, she still finds it necessary to import labour.

Indeed that necessity existed before the present war. Work begets work. In any case, Adolf Hitler's solution of the unemployment problem was a challenge which international finance could not ignore.

The success of the international Jewish conspiracy, supported also by corrupt and selfish non-Jews, depended on the magnitude of its scope. More than 80,000,000 of the most industrious and able people in the world were lifted by Hitler right out of the domain of the Hebrew system.

The whole conception, moreover, of international finance is repugnant to the National-Socialist.

He can see no argument for investing his country's capital abroad to the detriment of home industries. It may well be that the latter yield a lower dividend. In many cases, it is desirable that they should. The fair distribution of wealth is quite incompatible with unlimited profits.

But, even if an extreme case be taken, a National-Socialist would prefer to draw 2 per cent from a useful home industry rather than take 20 per cent from a foreign concern which competes with the labour of his fellow-workers.

The National-Socialist, conscious of race and tradition, deems it his duty to think, work, and spend for his country. The German National-Socialist, for example, finds it hard to understand why British financiers should have injured England's coal trade by placing their resources at the disposal of Polish coal mines in which sweated labour was employed.

In general, then, the National-Socialist theory is that the "money" which is made in a country should go to its further development, and that any temporary sacrifice is justified by the ultimate benefit that it will bring to his nation.

This view is so diametrically opposed to the whole thesis of international finance that there should be no difficulty in understanding why a conflict between the two could not be avoided.

Whether or not the conflict was to be armed was a matter that the international financiers themselves had to decide. They did not reach the decision to employ military force until every other method of beating Germany and frustrating Hitler had been tried and exhausted. Patiently they waited for the predicted collapse of the new German economic system. It never came, because their influence was ruled out from the first day. Then when unemployment vanished and production rose by leaps and bounds, they knew that waiting was useless.

Just as scores of previous wars were fought in the interests of their order, so a new war was launched. The Hebrews and their creatures had set out on the last desperate expedition to keep the world in bondage. The real masters of Britain had played their last card.

With this fraternity our next chapter deals.

Chapter VI: The Jews

THIS chapter had better begin with the intelligent criticism of the Jewish race by one of its own illustrious members, Israel Zangwill:

"Pious fanatical zealots, throttled by Talmud coil,
Impious, lecherous sceptics, cynical stalkers of spoil,
Wedded 'neath Hebrew awning, buried 'neath Hebrew sod,
Between not a dream of duty, never a glimpse of God.
Blarneying, shivering, crawling, taking all colours and none,
Lying, a fox in the covert; leaping, an ape in the sun."[86]

After this verdict, nothing that I have to write on the subject will seem too strong.

It is characteristic, indeed, of the Jewish superiority complex to make such a brazen admission of Jewish faults.

And, first of all, we must consider the Jewish character. It must, moreover, be considered in relation to race and not religion.

Whether the Jew is orthodox, atheist, or Christian, he remains a Jew. If he is orthodox, the path of his dishonesty may be slightly more predictable. When a Jew asks you to consider his case on religious grounds, he is merely trying to play on your sympathy, and using his faith for the same purpose as the *Kol Nidre*, that is to say the solemn forswearing of all vows that may be given in the year to come.

Thus, it is not proposed to examine here the question as to how far the Jewish religion may have influenced Jewish character. Those who accept the Old Testament as an authority will, if honest, come to the conclusion that no form of religion could be revealed to the Jews which they would not forthwith debase into materialism of the grossest order.

As Dryden says, they were

"A moody, headstrong, murmuring race
As ever tried the extent and stretch of grace."[87]

Adamantine materialism, a flair for assuming mysticism outwardly, a supreme contempt for other races, a complete disregard for other

[86] *Israel*, by Israel Zangwill. Joseph Friedlander, comp. *The Standard Book of Jewish Verse*. 1917.

[87] *Absalom and Achitophel*, by John Dryden, 1681.

peoples' rights, cleverness in imitation and improvisation, contempt for all labour not associated with high profits, great energy in the cause of money-making, a hatred of all nationalism but their own, a high degree of loyalty to their own family and their own community, an implicit faith in the power to corrupt Gentiles, a brilliant capacity for intrigue, and a pathetic inability to keep pace with any deeper thought or higher idealism are the chief characteristics of the Jewish race.

On all these attributes, volumes could be written: but it should suffice to express the resultant of these forces very simply in the following tendencies:

1. An incapacity to avoid forming a state within a state.

2. Complete inability to view their Gentile hosts as possessing equal rights with their own.

3. Predetermined specialisation in all those processes which bring high profit. Hence, in capitalism, almost exclusive preoccupation with finance, distribution, and exchange as distinct from productive industry. Professional work undertaken either for profit or for the sake of social advancement.

4. A natural tendency to utilize social and economic advancement for the purpose of gaining political power.

5. An unholy dread of nationalism as a factor which would draw attention to their racial nature and expose their operations.

6. The deliberate debasement of the standards of culture in the land of their sojourn.

7. The elimination by competition of the Aryan who merely wants to get enough for himself and not more than anybody else.

These resultants seem to manifest themselves in every land that the Jew inhabits. There can be no doubt that he is a hard worker, where there is profit to be made.

The German or the Englishman may think: "Well, now, I have done my day's work, and I can settle down to a little enjoyment." Not so the Jew. His only form of enjoyment is the gaining of power.

Whilst the white man works to enjoy something of life, the Jew works to become the master of his environment. When others are drinking their beer and chatting idly, he is cynically stalking his spoil.

This is, perhaps, one of his worst characteristics: I make no plea for laziness: but the thought that a man cannot settle down to enjoy some pleasure in life without having to reckon with the ever vigilant Hebrew is a horrible thought indeed.

Such a state of affairs means that all culture, all enjoyment, must give way to the ruthless pursuit of profit and pelf.[88] This factor has contributed more than is generally realized to the unpopularity of the Jewish race.

The Jew who reads this passage will probably exclaim: "Ha! Ha! I was right. They was jealous of the work us boys can do!"

This misunderstanding is typically Hebrew and relates to the purpose of life itself. If a Jewish coal-miner, could such a thing be found, decided to work two hours extra a day, nobody could have any objection, except a narrow-minded Trade Union Official.

But it is not in honest production that the Jews work overtime: it is always in some calling which enables profits to be made at the expense of others.

Just as the tendency to this form of competition arouses antagonism, so an even greater hostility is aroused by the natural Jewish practice of installing one's friends and relations in all accessible places of vantage.

Where Moses comes today, Rachel comes tomorrow, and the day after tomorrow there will arrive Isaac, Nathan, Benjamin, Ruben, Hyman, Levi, Hesther, Solomon, Isidore, and Samuel, with poor old Aaron panting in the rear, Talmud under his arm.

Give them a few months, and nothing short of a wholesale persecution can root them out, unless, of course a monetary revolution takes place, in which case the fraternity will start to dwindle as mysteriously as it appeared. Extreme poverty would have the same result. But the process of dwindling would not begin so long as a single Aryan was left to pluck.

As an illustration of the odious character of this race, I would quote the case of a Jewish student whom I was once compelled to teach. He had won the second scholarship awarded by a medical school in London. He was in tears. I asked him what was the matter with him. He replied that he was disappointed because he had not come first.

Such an attitude is not only thoroughly unhealthy but so far out of keeping with the character of the Teutonic races that it is extremely difficult to see how there can ever be an abiding peace between them and the Jews except by the exclusion or disappearance of the latter.

The communal spirit, the energy, the materialism of the Hebrews, their system of family education, the laws prescribed both by the

---

[88] Pelf: Money or wealth, especially when regarded with contempt or acquired by reprehensible means. From the from Old French *pelfre* (booty); related to Latin *pilāre* to despoil.

Talmud and their spoken tradition with regard to the treatment of the non-Jew have rendered it inevitable that they should accumulate a vast stock of the commodity called money.

It is only a superficial critic who supposes that they value money for its own sake. They are not mean. If they often save carefully and count their pennies, it is only because every Jew sees in cash the only means of power.

If the expenditure of 1 40,000 on a hospital buys a knighthood and a seat on the Board of Governors from which the appointment of other Jews to the staff can be suggested, the money is not begrudged.

If a Jew decides to entertain socially, he usually does so on a lavish scale. If a Jew gains the entrée to a country house and perceives that the estate is declining for lack of funds, he is quite likely to offer a loan without any stipulation as to repayment.

Later his son or daughter marries into the family, Nathan Klausenberg becomes Sir Nathaniel Clavering—country gentleman—and the loan is repaid by shares in the English Aristocracy Limited.

If only the Hebrew would use his pelf like a vulgar merchant, he would be easier to tolerate. Instead, he employs it to permeate into every stratum of society, carrying with him his racial consciousness, his racial character, his racial purpose, and his monstrous materialism.

In this way it has come about that a very large number of the so-called aristocratic families of Britain are impregnated with Oriental blood.

At the polite and select dinner table, it is never safe to discuss the Jews, because the family plate has probably been presented by the latest Jewish brother-in-law.

I remember one young English gentleman with a very ancient name who said to me one day: "I say, I hate the Jews, don't you?" I replied in the affirmative.

He said: "Yes! And the worst of it is that I can't talk about it at home, because my sister's married one of the beasts?"

The poor young man, if not already dead, is now in the armed forces of the Crown, fighting a Jewish battle.

This resentment of the creeping by Judah even into the family bed is deeply resented at heart: but the English aristocracy is both poor and demoralized. It has had to suffer so much that it is thankful to anybody who will give it a tip. The Jews, of course, have no more interest in developing estates than in bacon curing. They are merely delighted to become Masters of Foxhounds and Justices of the Peace, thereby extending their scope of corruption.

For corruption it is. It is a corruption designed to achieve a racial domination all the more objectionable because it has neither "a local habitation nor a name." A few years ago, it was a sin to mention the word "Jew" in British "Society".

Fortunately the position has changed. The Hebrews are mentioned freely enough and the day of reckoning is being prepared for them by the working classes, who have at last begun to identify their real rulers.

The poorer a man is, the better his chance of being anti-Jewish. He has nothing material to lose. If the rich attack the Jews, they may expect the sort of treatment meted out to Henry Ford, when he had to withdraw the famous articles in the *Dearborn Independent*.[89]

Any British Fascist who was working for a Jewish firm was dismissed as soon as his views were known. Such dismissals were not unnatural: but they serve to show the power which the Jew can exercise in countries which grant him hospitality.

So long as the idea of nationalism, arising from blood and inherited tradition, persists on this earth, the Jew can never be anything but an anti-social animal until and unless he is segregated.

He can never settle down in equilibrium in Western society. He can never be satisfied with a fixed share in the state. A Jew is either extending his influence or waiting for the undertaker: and if he does the latter, he probably asks for demurrage.

The unbearable attributes of the Jews were recognized in the thirteenth century by that great English King, Edward I. He expelled the lot. Gradually they began to creep back again, but were not admitted with a flourish until Cromwell's time.

Puritanism, breathing the quintessence of the Old Testament, was admirably suited to their needs: it served as a most useful suggestion of a community of interests between them and their hosts: and it

---

[89] Henry Ford (1863–1947), the founder of the Ford Motor Company. In 1920, he sponsored a weekly newspaper, the Dearborn Independent, which publicized Jewish tactics in business, politics and society. Every Ford franchise nation-wide carried the paper and distributed it to its customers, reaching over a million readers per week. The most important articles were published in a four volume book set known as *The International Jew*. A libel lawsuit was brought by a San Francisco Jew led Ford to close the *Independent* in December 1927, and allegedly recanted his views in a public letter to the Jewish Anti-Defamation League. In reality, Ford's retraction was not signed by him (his signature being forged by an aide) and he allowed the letter to go out to halt a Jewish-organized boycott of his business.

also disposed men towards that materialism which the Hebrews so thoroughly understood and knew how to exploit.

Gradually the stories of Hugh of Lincoln[90] faded out of the national consciousness: and the Jews became "a grand old people who gave us our religion." Again and again the leading prelates of the Church of England have made this statement during recent years.

So purblind are these ecclesiastical leaders that they do not see the humorous implication of their aphorism: yet, it is fairly obvious that if the Jews had valued Christianity highly, they would not have made a free present of it to the Church of England.

Sometimes, when I have seen some fat bishop waddling along, I have recalled his statements and assertions to the effect that the "Jews gave us Christianity," and, without pondering on the merits of the case, I have pictured the old devil dividing garments at dusk on Calvary.

During the nineteenth century, Jewish money-power was in the ascendant: and, as has been previously explained, its doctrines found a very receptive body of opinion in England.

As early as the Battle of Waterloo, the Rothschilds were exercising a decisive influence on the finance of the City. Throughout the century, their power increased: and, in the end, their country estates at Tring became the second seat of British government.

It is, however, a great mistake to suppose that Jewish interests in Britain are limited to the realms of finance. There, of course, they are supreme. They do not hold many bank directorships. But they do

---

[90] Little Saint Hugh of Lincoln (1246–1255) was an English boy murdered in what became known as one of England's most celebrated alleged ritual murders. The nine year old Hugh disappeared on July 31, 1255, and his body was discovered in a well on 29 August. It was claimed that a local Jew by the name of Copin had imprisoned Hugh, during which time he tortured and eventually crucified him. Copin was arrested and admitted to killing the child. As part of his confession, Copin claimed that it had been carried out with the acquiescence of the Jewish community. As a result, some ninety Jews were arrested and held in the Tower of London, while they were charged with involvement in the ritual murder. Eighteen of the Jews were hanged for refusing to participate in the proceedings. The remainder were pardoned and set free. The ritual murder allegation was dismissed as propaganda, but in 2007, an Italian Jewish professor of Medieval and Renaissance History at Bar Ilan University in Israel by the name Ariel Toaff (who was the son of Elio Toaff, former Chief Rabbi of Rome) published a book *Pasque Di Sangue* ("Passovers of Blood", Bologna, 2007) in which he argued that there was some truth to the so-called "blood libel." Toaff came under severe pressure, and within a week of publication, he ordered the book withdrawn, the offending passages removed and the book republished the following year without his original claims.

determine the price of gold. They do control the lending operations of the City: and such interests as those of the Rothschilds and the Sassoons are sufficiently powerful to smash the banks under the present system.

A threat to call in loans or to withdraw deposits can work wonders. Such threats have often been made. A more subtle influence can be exercised by the manipulation of stocks in such a fashion as to cause the greatest anxiety to banking-houses and investors alike.

Naturally, it would be possible to write many volumes on the subject of the various methods of crime peculiar to the City of London and similar institutions: it is only necessary, however, for the reader to appreciate the fact that when millions start moving in mass, they can derange any delicately balanced system of finance. The Jews are well aware of this fact and have always made use of it.

Moreover, their brothers and cousins, their uncles and aunts abroad are always willing to help them. Thus, in an unrestricted capitalist state of affairs, there is no difficulty in transferring money from one country to another. Nor is there any feature of Jewish activity more constant than the close cooperation of Hebrews in different lands.

Indeed, it is the possibility of this cooperation and its cash value that renders the Jews so violently opposed to nationalism. They take the whole of the world to be their province, as long as they are allowed to do so.

In this fashion, they have been able to fortify themselves against the collapse of the market in any one particular country. The Schiffs, the Warburgs, the Rothschilds, the Sassoons, the Ellermans, the Guggenheimers, the Cassells[91] regard themselves as international princes. For them the emergence of economic nationalism implies a fatal restriction on their operations.

Today, however, as above suggested, the territory of the Jew extends far beyond the bounds of impure finance in England. Emboldened by his success in this field, he has advanced to conquer the distributive trades and those branches of commerce most closely connected with the provision of the people's most vital needs. He has also invaded with overwhelming success the regions of film and press.

In fact, it should be of interest to note briefly the extent of the Jewish conquest in the provision trade, the furnishing trade, the clothing trade, the retailing of household goods, the chemical industry, the oil and petrol trade, housing, the press, the cinema, and finally the professions.

---

[91] All prominent Jewish banking and business families in America and Britain.

The Jewish power in England is all the more formidable because, until lately at least, it has been so carefully masked and kept in an obscurity which if not decent was effective.

Now, however, it is possible, by observing the above-mentioned categories, to dispel the illusion that the Jew is merely a patient old Shylock waiting in his dingy City Office to lend money to any Bassanio who can find an Antonio[92] to guarantee the necessary pound of flesh. Had the Jew remained in that position, he would be merely a commensurable pest. As it is, he has become an inescapable presence—an odious approximation—a haunting conscience—a shadow lengthening in the noon-tide of your prosperity—the ounce of sour in the pound of sweet—the fly in your ointment—and the Death's Head at your banquet.

In the provision and catering trade, the best known firm in Britain is that of Messrs. John Lyons. Who John Lyons was and what became of him must be a matter for lengthier research than I can afford. But the actual proprietors are as Jewish as anything that ever entered a synagogue.

The great chiefs rejoice in the names of Salmon and Gluckstein.[93] Perhaps the most important of their number is Sir Isidore Salmon,[94]

---

[92] Antonio and Bassanio are the two major characters in William Shakespeare's *The Merchant of Venice* (1598). In the play, Bassanio borrows money from Shylock the Jew to finance his expenditures as a suitor for Portia, using Antonio as the loan's guarantor. The two gentiles default on the loan, and thereafter follows the famous "pound of flesh" episode, in terms of which Shylock demands the right to payment in Antonio's life. He is prevented from cutting out a "pound of flesh" from Antonio by a clever legal ruse which argues that he only has rights to flesh, and not to blood—and that if he spills any blood in the act, he will be charged with attempted murder. Shylock is forced to give up his demand, and offers to settle for late payment with interest instead. This is however also denied to him because, under Venetian law, he as a Jew is an "alien" and because he has attempted to kill a Venetian, has forfeited his money to the state.

[93] J. Lyons & Co. was a British restaurant-chain, food-manufacturing, and hotel conglomerate founded in 1884, and only finally wound up in 1978. The company began as collaboration between the professional artist Joseph Nathaniel Lyons and his brothers-in-law, the Jews Isidore Gluckstein (1851–1920) and Montague Gluckstein (1854–1922), as a spin-off from the Salmon & Gluckstein tobacco company. J. Lyons & Co. was totally controlled by the Salmon and Gluckstein family.

94 Sir Isidore Salmon (1876–1941), Conservative Party Member of Parliament. The son of Barnett Salmon, cofounder of Salmon & Gluckstein tobacconists. From March 1938 until his death he held the office of "honorary catering adviser to the British Army," earning a fortune out of the contracts to supply food to the British Army. Also a vice-president of the Board of Deputies of British Jews.

Member of Parliament, who was discovered by the former Jewish War Minister, Hore-Belisha[95] to be the one man best qualified to take charge of the catering arrangements of the British Army.

The tobacco retailing firm of Salmon & Gluckstein is only one of the subsidiaries of John Lyons. This latter firm has its branches in every town of any importance in Britain. The first stage of success was its gradual elimination of the small British tea-shops, which could not compete with the power of massed capital and the favourable wholesale terms which Salmon and Gluckstein had at their disposal.

Then the scope of operations was extended to cover every kind of grocery and even meat. By scientific undercutting, the firm has manages to drive thousands of small traders into the bankruptcy courts.

John Lyons is not the only Jewish firm interested in groceries. The great Unilever combine, with a total capital of more than two hundred million pounds, embracing Lever's, Mac Fisheries, Lipton's, Sainsbury's, Home & Colonial, Maypole Dairies, and many similar concerns is under Jewish control.

Amongst the names to be found on the list of directors are such good old English patronymics as Jurgens, Schicht, Hartog, Rijkens, and Van den Berg. The altruistic interest of these people in providing England with food and soap is marvellous. The whole organization is riddled with Jews. For example, the Chairman of Home and Colonial is Sir George Schuster, a member of one of the most influential Hebrew

---

95 Leslie Hore-Belisha (1893–1957), a Member of Parliament for the Liberal and the Conservative party. He became Minister of Transport in 1934, and was then appointed Secretary of State for War in 1937, holding the post until 1940. He was deeply unpopular with the British public, and in the early months of World War II, a popular antisemitic song emerged to the tune of "Onward, Christian Soldiers". A version was recorded by Charlie and his Orchestra in Germany and was frequently played over propaganda broadcasts.
"Onward Conscript Army,
You have naught to fear.
Isaac Hore-Belisha,
Will lead you from the rear.
Clad by Monty Burton,
Fed on Lyons pies;
Fight for Yiddish conquests
While the Briton dies.
Onward conscript army,
Marching on to war.
Fight and die for Jewry,
As we did before."

families. He also finds time to act as Chairman of Maypole Dairies. Another subsidiary, the African and Eastern Corporation, dealing in margarine and soap, is Lieutenant-Colonel Beddington, another Jew. Beddington is related by marriage to the wealthy Behrens family, which has a large interest in the chain tailors—Montague Burton, Ltd.

On inspecting records in 1936, I found that amongst the prominent shareholders of the Unilever Combine were the Prudential Trust Corporation, Midland Bank, Barclays Bank, Mutual Insurance Co., Scottish Life Assurance, Alliance Insurance Co., and—Heaven help us!— British Widows Assurance.

If, then, anybody asks what connection banking and insurance have with Jewish interests, here is the answer. As between Lyons and Unilever, all is neatly planned, so that there is no destructive competition: but it is fantastic to suppose that the small-shopkeeper could compete for very long with gigantic sales machines of this order.

Once, however, the small man is completely eliminated, the public will be entirely in the grip of the big Jewish purveyors. When allowance is made for the fact that not only banks and insurance companies have hitched their wagons to the Star of Zion, but that also a very large number of Members of Parliament have done likewise, it is easy to see why no remedial legislation can be expected against any abuses which the victorious merchant princes may care to commit.

In London, Jewish control of public houses is on the increase: and the firm of Levy & Franks competes successfully with those taverns where the workman was in the habit of going for his "Joint and Two Veg." As yet, the development is only incipient, but it will proceed apace.

The furnishing trade has been going over to Judah for many years. A large part of the cabinet-making trade in London, Manchester, and elsewhere is in Jewish hands. In the East End of London, the proportion of Jewish control is not less than 80 per cent.

Meanwhile, the great hire-purchase firms get rid of the furniture, whether made by sweated labour in the slums or not. These firms spend thousands a week on advertisements. Smart Bros. Ltd., the best known, probably spends thousands a day in popularizing its wares by displaying in the press the various anatomical attitudes of a voluptuous young lady who is clad only in such places as are intended to arouse the curiosity of the male or Lesbian beholder. Mr. Hore-Belisha was Chairman of this firm until his presence in the Cabinet proved to be indispensable. Compelled by his acceptance of office to resign his chairmanship, he left his interests in the faithful hands of Messrs. Teller, Lynes, and Goldberg, who still traded under the name of Smart, despite the fact that their promoted colleague could no longer act as chief shop-walker. Smart they certainly are.

These hire-purchase firms employ, without scruple, all the devices of sales psychology to make the poor pledge themselves to exorbitant undertakings. In this respect, Smarts are no worse than the other Jewish firms, such as Bolsoms, Blundels, Wolff & Hollander, Jays, and Drages.

You may ask why they should aim at establishing debts which cannot be liquidated. The answer is that the real strategic aim is to establish a lien on the greater portion of the workers' wages. The nominal price of the goods is always far in excess of its ordinary cash retail worth. After a time, when instalments begin to lapse, a representative calls and threatens Court proceedings.

The woman of the house is dismayed. A pound a month did not seem much to pay for the radio. Two shillings a week for some blankets from Blundels seemed only a trifle, half a crown a week was evidently very cheap for the front-room suite which Messrs. Smarts pressed upon her, and then nobody could say that ten shillings a month for a piano represented greed on Sir Benjamin Drage's part.

Still, when all the tallymen came at once and threatened to see her husband, it was hard to know what to do. One tallyman, kinder than the rest says that he will consult his "directori." If she places a further order to the value of only a shilling a week and pays just a little on account—say two bob, Ma'am—County Court proceedings can be avoided. Times will improve, Ma'am.

So she pays the bloodmoney and gives the tallyman a cup of tea. Relaxing, and patting the little daughter on the head, he admires her fair hair, and then talks about his own children. Unless he gets so many new orders, he explains, each week, he will get the sack. His employers are Yids.

He is very sorry indeed that the good woman has so much trouble: but we all must live. Thankfully draining his tea and promising to come without fail on the following Monday, he goes ten yards down the street and repeats the process.

The noble "directors" do not mind. They are philosophers and they reflect that if one cannot get all one asks, the next-best thing is to get as much as possible. No good business man can hope to secure more than a legal lien on the workers' wages. If the furniture has to be confiscated because the instalments lapse, there is an army of Jewish polishers waiting to restore its lost youth preparatory to resale.

If the damage is too far gone, *Vell!* There is always antique shops, isn't there, Solly? Such was the scandal of hire-purchase that not long ago Miss Ellen Wilkinson delivered a slashing attack in the House of Commons upon its methods.

Little will come of her efforts. It is the whole nature of the system and its appeal that needs correction, not minor details or injustices. Sometimes the process is merely one of money-lending. Goods are taken by the very poor and pawned.

I once saw a talleyman handed a pawn-ticket by a woman who had not been able to redeem the goods in time. He kept it as security, well knowing that the day of reckoning must come. The pawnbroker could be compelled to part with the goods at any time. The wretched woman, however, was accumulating a double debt.

So much detail has been devoted to this one small aspect of Jewish business because it is typical of the whole and true to historic type. A number of these firms deal in clothes as well as furniture. Some add coal to the list. With these perishable or consumable goods, the talleyman must be more watchful. Here the arts of intimidation have to be practised with skill.

I know of one firm of this character which sent out a very official-looking final demand on portentous blue paper, the exact size of a Summons—headed with the legend, in Gothic type *County Court.*

Many ignorant people must have supposed that the law had been actually invoked against them. Where it is invoked, of course, the defendant must pay costs—often exceeding the amount of the debt. Failure to pay the sum stipulated by the Court may lead to committal to prison for an indefinite period.

It is very interesting to ask whether the suspense and fear in which hundreds of thousands of people in Britain are kept by these methods of trading are regarded by Parliament as evidence of the British love of freedom. Debt, the fear of unemployment or sickness and its economic results, a constant struggle to pay what cannot be found are the main features of the democratic freedom which the majority of the English people support.

Let us now turn to the clothing trade. The conditions which prevailed in the Jewish sweat-shops of East London and Manchester, to say nothing of Leeds, demanded Parliamentary legislation early in this century.

However, experience shows that there is no form of Parliamentary legislation which the Jews cannot circumvent. Everybody acquainted with the Yorkshire woollen industry knows exactly how the Jews entrenched themselves. Thus in Leeds today, there is a Hebrew population of approximately 50,000.

In consequence of these mighty efforts, it was possible for Jewish tailors to establish chain-stores all over the country. The most notorious firm so set up is that of Montague Burton. Whence the Montague came is another unsolved mystery. But Maurice and Bernard Burton are registered at Somerset House as Russians. They are no more Russians than your author is a Chinaman. They are Jews of the first and last water. Formerly they were called Orbach. But, in still earlier times, they must have had a more Biblical name.

As early as 1935, they had 500 branches in Britain and 364 other retail shops through Key Estates Ltd. The list of directors is not exactly Anglo-Saxon. It contains the names of Lord Greenwood (Hamar Grunewald), David Olinsky, Ellis Hurvitz, Baronich Huzoff, Beddington Behrens, and, of course, Maurice and Bernard. These persons have pursued an eminently successful war against the small British tailor and have, quite naturally, gained a number of contracts for the fighting forces. To make everything quite respectable, however, the chief clothing advisor to the British Forces of the Crown is one Sir Philip Marquess.

He is not yet entitled to sport strawberry leaves, but he is a Jewish gentleman of considerable initiative: and it is not too much to hope that one day he may become Lord Burton of Trent.

At any rate, in choosing the purveyors of food and clothes to the Services, Mr. Belisha could scarcely be accused of disloyalty to his own people.

These Jewish tailors are cordially hated by the British members of the trade: but, once again, heavy capital and good wholesale terms are decisive. It is a weak-minded Jewish tailor who cannot work his way, by a series of fires, from Whitechapel to Regent Street.

I once saw a little Jewish shop being cleared of nearly all its stock. Gown after gown was tucked away into one car after another. Fifteen minutes later the place was on fire: and all the stock was destroyed.

Curiously enough, when I saw the said gowns being loaded into the cars, I had a strong temptation to ring up the fire station. The more astute Jewish business man is usually a Little nervous about the fire-brigade.

One wealthy Jewish merchant in Richmond, Surrey, even went so far as to provide the Fire Brigade with accommodation between two and three miles outside of the town. The rural environment was good for the firemen—far better than the noisy urban surroundings which they had hitherto been obliged to support in Richmond.

There can be no doubt that the longer ride to work was just as good for the firemen as it was bad for the Insurance Companies. From their country seat, the members of the Brigade received far more calls than they had received in town.

The reason for this phenomenon could probably be explained by that great expert in pyrotechnics—Leopold Harris.[96]

In the retailing of household goods, the small British trader has had to yield before the sweeping advance of Messrs. Woolworths and the firm of Marks and Spencer. In 1935, Woolworths had 628 branches in Britain: and since then, the number has increased.

The capital was ten million pounds.

In 1931, N. M. Rothschild and Sons acquired 4,800,000 six per cent cumulative Preference Shares and 2,250,000 ordinary shares. Amongst the chief shareholders are H. V. Bevington, Jew, for N. M. Rothschild, a Sebag Montefiore, also Jewish, the Jewess Lady Baron, and Israel Moses Sieff, whose race is sufficiently indicated by his name and who is also the main proprietor of Marks and Spencers.

This latter firm is quite a menagerie. Mr. Spencer vanished long ago: but the business of the hundreds of stores belonging to the firm, with a capital of more than five million pounds, is controlled by Israel Moses Sieff, who has or had the able assistance of Luther Green, Simon Marks, Norman Laski, Alexander Isaacs and R. F. Nauheim.

The latter represents or represented the Industrial Finance & Investment Corporation Ltd, whose board is honoured with the names of Lord Melchett, the Jewish controller of Imperial Chemicals Ltd., P. Lindenberg, A. I. Belisha, M. Luebeck, and E. Spiegelberg.

Amongst the chief shareholders of Marks & Spencers in 1936 were the following: Prudential Insurance Comp any (also a shareholder in the Polish mines); Ephraim Sieff; Theo Gluckenheimer; B. Weizman;

---

[96] In July 1933, the Jew Leopold Harris, was named as an arch-conspirator in a sensation trial of a gang in London which became known as the "fire-rasiers." Harris, a trained fire assessor, specialized in setting fires and claiming from insurance companies through various fronts. Harris was sentenced to 14 years' imprisonment.

Loewenstein & Hecht; Mrs. Sacher; S. Japhet & Co.; P. Linberg; Swiss Bank Corporn.; Sir Max Michaelis; Scottish National Trust; Gaston Mendel; B. Isaacs; Julius Sern; Mrs. E. Laski; S. S. Cohen; Alex Isaacs; Sara Laski; Nathan Laski; Paul Loewi; Herman Loewi; Ephraim Marks; Simon Marks; Rebecca Sieff; Lena Marks; B. I. Werzman; Israel Moses Sieff; M. Luebeck; Singer & Friedlander; Marcus, Harris, & Lewis; Noah Laski; National Bank of Scotland; Miriam Marks; J. A. Cohen; Mathilda Marks; Otto Loevi; Alec Cohen; and Mrs. Emily Isaacs.

These data were available when I last inspected the records. By this time the happy family ought to have grown.

Attention must again be directed to the connection between this Jewish enterprise and the world of banking and insurance. It is not necessary for Mr. Israel Moses Sieff to sit on the Board of the Bank of England in order to have his way. He need only wag a finger in the Board Room of Marks & Spencers in order to make the banks tremble.

Woolworths and Marks & Spencer sell all sorts of household goods, garden hoses, soap, hardware, fittings, gramophone records, as well as ice-cream and cosmetics.

Indeed it is very difficult to mention any line of small business with which they do not compete. As Mr. Israel Moses Sieff is on the board of both companies, there is no danger of serious competition between the two. Backed by at least fifteen million pounds capital, favoured with the best wholesale terms and unlimited credit, skilled in seeking out the cheapest labour markets of the world, they can run the small shopkeeper off the street.

They employ female labour: and it is by no means uncommon in some of these stores for a girl of 18 or 19 to work 60 or 70 hours a week for very low pay. The atmosphere is usually foul and the attendant must be on her feet all day, snatching a meal as best she can. Thus, despite the low prices charged, the profits are enormous, so that Sara, Lena, Miriam, and Rebecca do not have to think of the white shopgirls who ruin their health and, not infrequently, their morals in the great task of building Jerusalem in England's green and pleasant land.[97]

The low purchasing power of the people naturally urges them to buy as cheaply as possible, without regard to the manner in which the cheapness has been attained.

---

[97] A reference to the poem "And did those feet in ancient time" by William Blake (1804). Today it is best known as the anthem "Jerusalem" with the lines "I will not cease from Mental Fight, Nor shall my Sword sleep in my hand: Till we have built Jerusalem, In England's green & pleasant Land."

A considerable part of the goods offered has been made by cheap Oriental labour: but the purchasers are not politicians: they buy what they can: and whether they ruin British traders or throw British workers out of employment is immaterial to them when they see something cheap. This is exactly the frame of mind that democracy induces. Hence its invaluable utility to the Jewish exploiter.

It would be possible to give other examples of this type of Hebrew enterprise: but the two instances cited should be enough.

It is easy to say that the British trader should defend himself: but it is hard to see how he can do so without going to the length of revolution. In democracy, he has no means of making his opinion known, much less respected. He cannot go, like Lady Sieff, and have a cosy chat with the Royal Family.

Consequently, the decline of the individual trader has been very marked in recent years: given another ten years, the Jewish magnates could probably cause him to disappear altogether. At any rate, the struggle has been a losing one for English tradesmen: and the sad fact is that many of them have been at a loss to understand why business was so bad.

Concerning the chemical industry, it is sufficient to mention the fact that the Melchett interests are predominant in Imperial Chemical Industries, the most important chemical undertaking in Britain.

Its Intelligence Department is somewhat better than those of the Government: but naturally there is much cooperation and overlapping between the former and the latter.

The present Lord Melchett had, for business reasons, been brought up as a Christian by his father, old Alfred Mond. He decided, however, a few years ago that it was fashionable to be Jewish and reverted to the faith of his fathers. The Mond interests are so widely spread that it would be impossible to trace them here.

The old man, however, was mainly interested in preventing the Dead Sea Salts from being developed on the basis of maximal production: and the story of how he and other Hebrews, including Leopold Amery,[98] managed the House of Commons in order to secure that tenders and

---

[98] Leopold Amery (1873–1955) was a half Jewish Member of Parliament and later Conservative government minister. His son, John Amery (1912–1945) was an early British fascist who, like the author of this book, defected to Germany at the beginning of the war and helped create a small British SS unit known as the British Free Corps, and also made recruitment efforts and propaganda broadcasts for Nazi Germany. He was arrested and executed by the British after the war.

contracts should go to low producers forms a very interesting chapter of Parliamentary History. The details of the swindle would require a whole volume.

In the petrol and oil industry, it is probable that Waley-Cohen and Lord Bearsted, formerly Montague, are the most powerful men in Britain today. Between them they hold more than a hundred directorships on the boards of oil and petrol companies. Their interests extend from Persia to Texas.

As has already been mentioned, the service of their private interests precluded the development of the oil from coal process in Great Britain, except on a quite contemptible scale.

In housing, too, the Jews are taking an increased interests. The main Portsmouth road is plastered with garish slogans advising the homeless to repose their confidence in Nathan Berg. In London recently certain blocks of flats have been adorned with the legend: "No Gentiles Need Apply." The Jews are certainly beginning to feel at home in their New Jerusalem.

We now come to the very interesting question of the British Press. In England it is fashionable to pretend that the Jews have nothing to do with it. The Hebrew influence however well concealed, is very strong. Papers like the *Times* and *Telegraph* which represent the high financial interest are naturally dependent on the goodwill of the City. That is to say, they must give the Jews most-favoured-nation treatment.

The Walters and the Astors of the *Times* are, of course, not Jewish: but their financial interests are those of Judea. Lord Camrose, of the *Daily Telegraph* claims to be Welsh. His origin is even more obscure than his business methods: but he is certainly connected by marriage with the Rothschild family: and his chief coadjutor, Colonel Lawson, is the descendant of Levi Lawson, later Lord Burnham, the founder of the paper.

These two well-known journals depend, like all other British dailies, upon advertisements. The continental reader may not understand to what an extent this dependency exists in England. No big paper can pay its way on its sales receipts in Britain. Rather, it would be possible to give a whole issue away free without a second thought, provided that the advertisement revenue were satisfactory: but a great percentage of this revenue is provided by the large Jewish firms such as Lyons and Smarts. The Jewish advertiser need only threaten to withdraw his advertisements in order to cause complete panic in the board-room of the paper in question. A good instance of the use of this power occurred, within my personal knowledge, in 1934. In the January of that year, Lord Rothermere, the chief proprietor of the *Daily Mail,* began to support Sir Oswald Mosley and his British Union of Fascists. He was generous both with his publicity and with his money. Very soon, however, he began to express grave concern at the growing anti-Jewish tendency of the movement—a tendency for which I was very largely responsible.

After a few months, he announced that he could support the Union no longer, unless it could be guaranteed that the movement would not be anti-Jewish and would abandon certain important parts of its policy. An open exchange of letters took place between him and Mosley, in which Lord Rothermere laid emphasis on the fact that he could not be a party to any anti-Jewish propaganda.

Actually, he admitted in private that Sir Isidore Salmon had told him that continued support of the British Union of Fascists would mean the withdrawal of all Lyons's advertisements from the *Daily Mail,* as well as any other financial inconveniences which could be arranged. Rothermere had thirty million pounds and could have stood the struggle. His directors, however, were prepared for no such sacrifice; especially reluctant was Mr. Szarvasy, a Jew himself, to disappoint the expectations of Sir Isidore.

Thus a multi-millionaire and a man of very strong character was compelled to bow down to the dictate of Jewry: and if he was not in a position to resist, who was? Whatever opinions may be entertained concerning Mosley and his movement, there could be no graver stigma on the so-called freedom of expression said to prevail in Britain than that a body of Englishmen should be prevented from expressing their views by an Oriental confectioner.

The patient Jewish reader must not, however, suppose that we are finished at this point with the Hebrew control of Britain's Press. A few names can be cited to show that much of this control is direct.

First on the list comes the super-Capitalist proprietor of the Socialist *Daily Herald* and Odham's Press, Ltd. This is Lord Southwood. The *Jewish Yearbook* for 1938 gives his earlier name as Julius Salter Elias. He is himself a Conservative and plays a kindly part in the functions of the local Conservative party in Fernhurst, where his sumptuous country mansion is situated. He seems to have every quality except poverty to conduct and control the main Socialist newspaper of Great Britain. His leading shareholder is one Abraham Abrahams, who cannot trace his descent to the Manchu dynasty.

My Lord Southwood controls scores of periodicals, including, funnily enough, *Sporting Life*. Those journals of high Society, the *Tatler* and the *Spectator* and the *Illustrated London News* are also his.

What a liberal-minded man it is who can depict in one paper the sufferings of the poor and in a half dozen others the extravagant festivities of the rich! One is tempted to think that His Lordship's breadth of mind is second only to his appreciation of sound profits.

One of his vice-Chairmen is Camille Akerman, another Jew, who is also a Trustee and Director of the *News Chronicle*. Somewhere in the background of this amusing journal there lurks a Hebrew accountant, one Hyman Binder, whose peregrinations through the *Stock Exchange Year-book* are so elusive as to baffle all but the most pertinacious inquirers.

Our noble Julius also owns the *Argus Press,* a piece of pelf that he managed to salvage from the wreckage of the *Morning Post.* A comradely interest is taken in Illustrated Newspapers, Ltd., by another shining light of Israel, Sir John Ellerman, son and heir of the worst ship-owner that ever lived.

Sir John, with the help of Israel Moses Sieff, conducts the pornographic and pornological horrors *The Daily Mirror* and the *Sunday Pictorial.* These wretched things exist for the purpose of stimulating hatred of Hitler and sexual activity at the same time.

The truest statement ever published in them was one in which a "medical expert" informed his readers that their brains consisted of 84 per cent water and 16 per cent grey matter. Each number tries to surpass the former in exhibiting the pectoral and fundamental aspects of woman: and I remember one issue which published a picture of a young lady lying on a couch accompanied by a letter from the damsel in question, stating that she was very lonely and giving her address.

Of course, there is nothing that the Jews so dearly love to market as a white woman's body. Even eighteen years ago, the *Jewish World* admitted that 75 per cent of the white-slave traffic was in Hebrew hands. Today the percentage is probably higher.

In the theatre and the film world, outside of Germany and Italy, the actress's easiest way to fame is through the bed-room of the Jewish manager. True to the Talmud, the Jew respects his own women and guards them tenderly: but his attitude towards all others is either greedily sensual or purely commercial, according to the circumstances. The managing director of the *Daily Express* is the veteran Jew, R. D. Blumenfeld, who is one of the most powerful members of the community in England. No doubt he has a hard nut to crack in Lord Beaverbrook: and it is not unlikely that they both have a share in moulding the paper's policy.

Between them, then, Elias, Ellerman, Lawson, Sieff, Akerman, Szarvasy, and Blumenfeld are able to exercise a decisive and direct influence on the British Press: but it must not be forgotten that if they all sold out, the power of advertisement revenue and the general control of finance would still be strong enough to ruin any newspaper that dared to face the Jewish question frankly.

In the film industry, the Jewish control is supreme, not only in England but also in the United States. In England, the Ostrers and Oscar Deutsch of Odeon renown are the great magnates. The former control not only Gaumont British and Fox films, but also the Baird television process.

The "Scophony" television company is controlled by Oscar Deutsch, Arthur Levey, and Solomon Sagall.

A young actor of my acquaintance, Maurice Braddell, took an interest in politics. For a time, he was a National-Socialist. It was made clear to him that unless he renounced this interest and its accompanying activity, he need expect no more contracts for either stage or screen. He even had to write a letter to the *Jewish Chronicle* disavowing what the Jew likes to call "anti-Semitism."

An interesting illustration of how the Jews use their control of the films is afforded by the following passage from the *Sunday Dispatch* of March 5, 1939: "Put glory into war pictures! Hollywood gets its orders." Hark at this: "Anti-war angles of the play are considerably softened and made more palatable for the masses.

This is part of an American critic's review of the film 'Idiot's Delight' . . . That's not really so surprising in view of the news from America that the U.S. Government has hinted to Hollywood that pacifist films are out and that death-or-glory pictures are to be preferred.

The fact is that the heads of the Government don't want a great propaganda medium to be preaching peace-at-any-price during these days of war talk all over the world." Needless to say, the great majority of the American public desired peace as heartily as anybody else in the world. What the above extract really means is that Mr. Churchill's patron,

Barney Baruch, together with Brandeis, Frankfuerter, Morgenthau, and the rest of the boys gave their co-racialists in Hollywood the eagerly awaited command to let slip the dogs of war. Such a candid statement could, however, hardly be expected from the *Sunday Dispatch*.

Whilst on the subject of propaganda, we must refer, in parentheses, to the slimiest of Hebrews, Victor Gollancz, who with his Left Book Club and his publishing house, did as much for the cause of war as the Ostrers with their poisonous "news-films."

In the professions, the gravest attack has been made on that of the doctor. Even as early as July 1935, 300 Jews from Germany had been admitted to practise medicine and surgery, and 200 to practise dentistry. Now, of course, the number must be huge. In Glasgow University alone there are 500 Jewish students.

According to the *Jewish Year-book* for 1938, more than 90 of the principal teaching posts in the Universities of Britain are held by Jews. But the Year-book refers only to Hebrews of the orthodox variety: therefore the actual number of Jews directing higher education must be greater.

Presently, we shall revert to the conditions created in England by the so-called "refugees." First, however, we must contemplate a little picture drawn by Lord Beaverbrook, under the nom-de-plume "Barnabe Rich" in the *Evening Standard* of May 27, 1939:

"There are Jews of prominence in the City. But not so many as you would expect, considering their financial ability . . . As for the world of Society, the Jews there are not many. But they play a prominent part. The foremost Jew in London is Sir Philip Sassoon. The walls of his Park Lane home are lined with valuable pictures . . . Sir Philip's sister, Lady Cholmondeley, is the leading Society Jewess . . . Sir Philip Sassoon's cousin, Mr. Edward Esmond, plays a part in racing and golfing society, both in London and in Paris. He made a fortune out of jute . . . Ted Esmond's surname used to be Ezra . . . Lord Rosebery, a half-Jew, owned the winner. Lord Melchett has been in Society, but has not stayed the course because he did not wish to do so . . The Rothschilds could be in Society if they wanted (!). Lionel prefers to exercise his importance in the outer world rather than the Society world. James is not in Society at all. He does not like going to parties . . . Tony is to some extent a Society figure, though seldom seen. Of the other full Jews in Society there is Mrs. Robert Lutyens, who before her marriage was called Eva Lubrzynski. She is a niece of Dr. Weizmann . . . Then there is Mrs. Mariot, daughter of Otto Kahn . . . Mrs. Venetia Montague and Lady Rothschild, who shine in Society today, are Jewesses, though not racially so. Both have professed Jewry . . . Mr. Lionel Montagu is another full Jew who is a first rate figure in Society. His presence is greatly sought after for week-end parties . . . A new Jewish figure is emerging and going up in London Society. That is the figure of Mr. Hore-Belisha. He has none of the antecedents which make for success in my world, but he brings with him agreeable manners and ability. No big party in Society is complete without his name. Now I come to the half-Jews in society . . . First in the list are brother and sister, Lord Rosebery and Lady Crewe . . . Sir John Fitz-Gerald, the twenty-first knight of Kerry, is a half-Jew. Then there is Lady Louis Mountbatten, granddaughter of Sir Ernest Cassel, and her sister, Mrs. Mary Ashley. Lady Brecknock is a half-Jewess . . . Among the quarter-Jews in Society, I select two women as leaders . . . First of all the Duchess of Roxburghe. She is Lady Crewe's daughter . . . Second quarter-Jew on my list is Mrs. Charles Wood, daughter-in-law of Lord Halifax . . . Mrs. Wood's husband, Mr. Charles Wood, is Member of Parliament for York. He is destined for success in Society and in politics, too. It is fair to say that the intelligence of his wife, as well as the fact that he is heir to the House of Halifax, will contribute to his success . . . Well, I have mentioned several Jews in Society."

So he has, this Captain Barnabe Rich, alias Beaverbrook. His little list refers only to fashionable "Society" with a capital S, and not to the section of the aristocracy which holds aloof from Mayfair.

His interesting catalogue gives no idea of the extent to which the older families have been permeated with the Hebrew taint.

Nor does he mention people on the fringe of Society, like Lord Camrose, who are connected with the Jews by marriage.

In every direction, the Jewish advance has been immensely strengthened by the influx of the so-called "refugees." If England had started banning the worst form of German export five years ago instead of in 1939, she would have saved herself the mortification of being eaten out of house and home by the new arrivals.

They have been shown preference before the Englishman to an extent inconceivable to those unacquainted with the facts and comprehensible only to those who appreciate at its true value the power of Jewry in England. So great has been the indignation of certain sections of the public that even the Press has had to take notice of the abuses which have arisen. The more farseeing Jews also have been quite worried as to the danger of the reaction which the behaviour of this new Army of Occupation must provoke.

The *Sunday Express* of October 23, 1938 wrote as follows:

"There are more aliens living and working in Britain to-day then ever before, and every day more are landing to swell the army. In May—the last month for which figures are available at the Home Office—the number of aliens registered with the police of England and Wales alone was 196,852 over the age of sixteen. In addition, of course, there are thousands in Scotland and Ireland. Since these figures were compiled there has been a big influx of Austrian refugees. We are now seeing the first wave of what may possibly be a much larger influx from Czecho-Slovakia . . . It costs only £10 to become British. In six months this year the total number of aliens naturalised has almost reached the total for the whole of the year 1937 . . . How do refugee aliens make a living? Once they obtain a permit to work from the Ministry of Labour they receive the same privileges and, incidentally, the same unemployment benefit as British subjects . . . aliens who can hardly speak English are now driving London taxicabs and forcing British drivers off the streets. Cut-price gown shops are also being opened right and left by aliens. Often they start by employing British sales girls who are later displaced by newly arrived foreigners often disguised—to get over regulations—as relatives. Influential aliens do not hesitate to put pressure on British firms to employ foreigners . . . Dr. A. Welply, secretary of the Medical Practitioners' Union, says: "I have investigated personally cases of threatening letters sent to doctors on hospital staffs who have opposed the admission of foreigners as colleagues. There have been cases of the dismissal of a British doctor without adequate explanation to make room for an alien of no better qualifications. There are hospitals now almost entirely staffed by alien doctors. . . Domestic servants, of course, form a huge proportion of the alien army in this country.""

Of course, the word "Jew" is carefully avoided in the above passage: but of course these "refugees" are not South-Sea Islanders: and one can hardly expect complete frankness from the British Press: indeed it is highly probable that no reference would be made to the invasion, were it not that silence might be construed as complicity.

Although the reader must now be growing a little weary of quotations, it is desirable to give just a few more, before bringing the subject to a close. Probably the most remarkable advertisement that ever appeared in a British newspaper is the following, taken from the *Times* of April 5, 1939:

"To Jewish refugees. Business man is prepared to finance establishment of new business or industry. Write in confidence to Box. M 132, *The Times*, E. C.1."

If some good man of means had offered to set up in business British ex-Servicemen who had grown tired of standing in unemployment queues, the readers of the Times would doubtless have been surprised.

But this remarkable offer probably aroused little curiosity except from the Nathans and Solomons who penned their confidential applications with kindled hopes.

When one thinks, however, of all those unfortunate Englishmen who have been waiting many years for such an invitation, one does not know whether to pity them or to condemn them as idiots for their failure to grapple with the menace in their land.

The *Evening Standard* of April 14, 1939 carried a half-page advertisement which read:

"2/6 will keep a refugee child safe for a day. 17/6 will keep a refugee child safe for a week."

The appeal, which had the blessing of Lord Baldwin and the Archbishop of Canterbury, did not remind the public of the fact that the child of an unemployed Englishman was supposed to be "kept safe" on 3/- a week. Exactly why a Jewish child should be deemed worth six times the value of an English child was not explained: but the valuation speaks for itself. It would be possible to multiply almost indefinitely the examples that we have given. Space, unfortunately does not permit.

Even the revenues of the hospitals have suffered through Jewish competition: and according to the *Catholic Herald* of March 24, 1939, many appeals which were to have been launched for them have been abandoned, in order that nothing might interfere with the flow of cash into the pockets of the Jewish invaders.

Callisthenes, Selfridge's chief publicist, reveals the full measure of Jewish modesty when he writes (*Times*, February 24, 1939): "Germany cannot strip herself of her leading industrialists—most of whom have Jewish affiliations—without laying herself open to the gravest hurt. Let England, then, acquire what Germany is losing."

Time may well prove "The stone which the builders rejected" to be "the headstone of the corner." There is a curiously Masonic ring about this piece of impudent publicity. According, however, to the *Daily*

Express of February 10, 1939, the National Federation of Grocers stated: "We can say without hesitation that aliens are responsible for cut-price trading, and that it has increased since refugees began to reach this country in large numbers.

These traders sell proprietory lines at cut-prices and, having attracted custom to their shops, unload cheap and unreliable goods on the housewives of this country . . . The trouble is that these people often have as many as a dozen aliases. No sooner have we stopped them trading under one name than they carry on under another."

On January 13, 1939, Mr. Dummett, the Bow Street Magistrate, said in Court: "This system by which Jews get sailors to smuggle them into this country, and then refuse to give the name of the ship or men who got them here, is a grave breach of the Aliens Act."

Mr. Metcalfe, the Old Street Magistrate, expressed himself on the subject in even stronger terms. Most of the stipendiary magistrates know that the so-called aliens are Jewish criminals of the lowest and shiftiest type or, at the best, rapacious political nuisances.

The resentment which is occasioned by the operations of these pestiferous harpies prompted Sir Samuel Hoare to say, in the House of Commons, on November 21, 1938: "In this country we are a very thickly populated industrial community with at the present a very large number of unemployed. Competition is very keen with foreign countries, and it is difficult for many of our fellow-countrymen to make a livelihood at all and keep their industries and businesses going. It is quite obvious that there is an underlying current of suspicion and anxiety, rightly or wrongly, on any big scale. I know from my own daily experience at the Home Office . . . that there is the making of a definite anti-Jewish movement. I do my best as Home Secretary to stamp upon an evil of that kind. That is why I have prohibited demonstrations in certain parts of London where they would inevitably stimulate this evil movement . . . I may be pardoned if I choose to pay tribute to the Jewish people, the race which we know better than any other race."

After delivering himself of this sickly oration, Sir Samuel could take additional pleasure in the luncheons which Sir Philip Sassoon used to give the Cabinet every Wednesday after its meeting. The most remarkable feature of his remarkable statement was the pleasure with which he announced his restriction of the liberty of His Majesty's subjects to utter their political opinions. After giving the grounds for the prohibition of this immigration, he calmly stated his intention of stamping on the British people if they dared to oppose it. His words sufficiently establish the argument which this chapter was intended to develop—namely the thesis that the Jews wield tremendous power in England.

For years the Government has tolerated huge Communist demonstrations against itself. Police have been battered about, the Union Jack has been torn to pieces in the streets, men have lain down on the busy streets and interrupted the traffic, thousands of people have been allowed to assemble and pelt the Fascists with stones and old iron. The House of Commons itself has been raided by the unemployed: but once let anybody of citizens try to demonstrate in their own streets against the menace of Jewry—and the case is altered. All fine phrases about democratic liberty are forgotten in the twinkling of an eye.

Thus it follows that the Jews have more influence than any other element in the population of Britain: and the strength which they possess is amply demonstrated by the facts given in the preceding pages.

Nothing like a comprehensive survey of the whole question would have been possible in so little space: but in view of the evidence adduced, it cannot be denied that the Jewish race had the opportunity to use England as the instrument of its policy: it had, moreover, the inclination, arising not only from its feud with Germany but from its essential opposition to the principles of National-Socialism. The inclination and the opportunity must be viewed together.

It must also be remembered that the Jewish conflict with Germany arose from the fundamental incompatibility between their concept of life and that of the Third Reich. They believed, and rightly, that the withdrawal of Central Europe from their system would damage irreparably that system itself. If persons of energy and tenacity be given the opportunity of executing a design arising from the strongest of motives, psychology teaches that they will execute it. The motive, in this case, was the destruction of National-Socialist Germany: and the opportunity lay in the enormous influence which they had acquired both economically and politically over Great Britain.

In the Press, with their films, both with the written word and with the spoken, they pursued their design with indefatigable assiduity. The full consequences of their crime are not yet to be appreciated. But the blood of those who fall in this war is on their hands, and on the hands of the contemptible politicians whom they made their tools in this nefarious enterprise. They have deliberately set their supremacy above the peace and the welfare of the world. In their incitement to war against Germany, they have shown neither regard nor pity for the suffering and the loss of life which this conflict must cause.

As they have acted, so must they be judged. Without remorse they have worked for the death of innumerable men. It is only fitting, in the circumstances, that they should pay the full penalty of their unscrupulous ambition.

When the clouds of war have rolled away, when the British people have been delivered up to the agonizing aftermath of this final conflict, when the world can behold what ruins the crime has produced, when hungry women and homeless children stare into the greyness of the future, the architects of evil themselves shall not survive.

On September 3, 1939, Britain declared war on Germany. But over and above this decree was another—a decree pronounced by the Supreme Court of History: it was the sentence of death upon the power, the riches, and the ambition of the Jewish race.

When this sentence will be executed, no man can say: but sooner or later, the most influential Jew on earth will have no more influence on the course of Aryan affairs than a jelly-fish upon the time of sunrise.

What the English people do not see today, they will learn by bitter experience: the German people have seen the truth already.

When twilight falls on the field of battle, it is the twilight of the Kingdom of Judah on earth.

They have tempted God—these Jews—for the last time.

Chapter VII: The Empire

IT is only a presumptuous person who would attempt to discuss the subject of the British Empire in a few pages. However, a close study of the people whom we discussed in the last chapter renders an attitude of presumption almost unavoidable: and, whilst the mood lasts, we might as well take advantage of it.

It is not my purpose to indulge in recriminations or to recite a list of England's dark deeds in the past. The British Empire was, in the main, formed by acts of armed force: and, from the many campaigns fought in order to achieve its creation, it is not possible to dissociate the cruelties which so often accompany wars of conquest.

In this respect, however, England does not stand alone. The history of the formation of the Roman Empire, the Holy Roman Empire, and many other empires is a record of violence and often ruthlessness.

It is only when England's politicians assume the white mantle of virtue and sanctimoniously claim an immaculate certificate of humanity for everything connected with British Imperial history or when they accuse other nations of gaining their ends by force that one has to observe politely but firmly that England's record in Ireland, Africa, India, North America, Malta, China, and Palestine stops her from criticizing those who may choose to employ military force in pursuit of their objectives.

The rights and wrongs of each case are beyond discussion here. Suffice it to say that even during the present century British Governments have used considerable force in South Africa,[99] India, Palestine, and

---

[99] References to: (1) The Second Anglo-Boer War of 1899–1902, during which the British rounded up the entire civilian Boer population in the Orange Free State and Transvaal into concentration camps. In those camps, in excess of 28,000 women and children died of starvation and disease—about 12 percent of the entire white population. (2) The autocratic rule of India by Britain, and the The Jallianwala Bagh massacre, also known as the Amritsar massacre, of April 1919 in particular. On April 13, a crowd of non-violent protesters, along with Baishakhi pilgrims, had gathered in the Jallianwala Bagh garden in Amritsar, Punjab to protest against the arrest of two of their leaders by the British. The army fired on the crowd for ten minutes, directing their bullets largely towards the few open gates through which people were trying

Ireland.[100] For whatever purpose it may have been employed, it has been used with sufficient frequency and vigour to warrant the judgement that England is prepared to realize her aims by military force without regard to the weakness or the wishes of those peoples against whom it is employed.

Thus, for example, if it be said that Russia invaded Poland only because the morals of the poor, innocent Commissars had been corrupted by the wicked Nazis, the wicked Nazis themselves had been corrupted by reading, in their youth, the exploits of Raleigh, Marlborough, Clive, Hastings, Wellesley, Napier, Codrington, Roberts, Rhodes, Jameson, Kitchener and Wolseley, to say nothing of Hawkins, Mountjoy, Carew, and Oliver Cromwell.[101]

A serious study of these biographies by apt pupils should leave one gasping at the modesty of the military measures that Germany has recently taken in Europe. Presumably, however, Sir John Hawkins[102] founded the slave trade in the sacred cause of democracy: Mountjoy[103] and Carew[104] decimated the Irish population in the interests of small nationalities: and there can be little doubt that Kitchener's drastic

to run out. The figures released by the British government were 370 dead and 1200 wounded. Other sources place the number dead at well over 1000. (3) The British rule of Palestine during the 1930s, which saw the League of Nations mandate used to further the Zionist seizure of that territory from the native Palestinian population. The British used military force to quell all Arab protests and uprisings against the Zionist interlopers.

[100] A reference to the centuries-long occupation of Ireland by the British, and the escalation of armed conflict between Irish republicans and the British army during the first 25 years of the 19th Century into a full-blown war. This conflict ultimately resulted in Britain partitioning Ireland and granting the larger part of the island nation independence.

[101] All figures from English history associated with either warfare, plundering, ransacking, invasion or the exploitation of foreign nations.

[102] Admiral Sir John Hawkins (1532–1595) was an English naval commander and administrator, merchant, navigator, shipbuilder, privateer and slave trader. He is considered the first English trader to profit from the Triangle Trade, based on selling supplies to colonies ill-supplied by their home countries, and their demand for African slaves in the Spanish colonies of Santo Domingo and Venezuela in the late 16th century.

[103] Charles Blount, 8th Baron Mountjoy and 1st Earl of Devonshire (1563–1606), who served as Lord Deputy of Ireland under Queen Elizabeth I, then as Lord-Lieutenant of Ireland under King James I. In 1600, Mountjoy went to Ireland and, with the assistance of Sir George Carew, brought the Nine Years War to an end with ruthless scorched-earth tactics.

[104] George Carew, 1st Earl of Totnes (1555–1629), served under Queen Elizabeth I during the Tudor conquest of Ireland and was appointed President of Munster.

treatment of the Boers in the closing stages of the South African War was merely intended to provide that mortification of the flesh which disposes the spirit the more readily to grasp the celestial mysteries of international finance.

On the other hand, I have no wish to conceal from the reader the fact that I was brought up to admire and honour the British Empire.

I saw in it an immense potentiality for good, if properly used: so, obviously did the Führer. More than once he has paid a tribute to some of England's Imperial achievements: and even in his famous speech of October 6, 1939, he showed no hostility to the concept of a British Empire. On the contrary, he made a most generous offer of recognition.

It is therefore outside the competence of my critics to say that, in this chapter, I am stating an *ex parte* case against the Empire's existence. On the contrary, I believe that every genuine movement of integration is a real advance in civilization.

A large system of units organized into true cooperation is just as beneficial to world peace as a large number of little units, squabbling amongst themselves, must be dangerous. If the British Empire were an honest unity, its dismemberment could not react favourably on world affairs.

The pertinent charge, however, against the British politicians is not that they are grasping Imperialists but that they have no conception of Imperialism at all. Certainly they juggle with one quarter of the world's surface and one fifth of its population under the delusion that they are managing an Empire; but, in fact, thanks to their greed and their materialism, the British Empire of today is merely a geographical expression.

The whole tragedy of the Empire lies in the democratic preference for extensity over intensity.

The great portion of the earth over which King George VI, Defender of the Faith, rules has not been economically developed to more than 10 per cent of its available capacity for development.

Yet there is starvation of the most abominable nature in India, there is unemployment in Britain, and 55 per cent of the total population of the Colonial Empire is suffering from malnutrition.

England had the opportunity of developing intensively the greatest estate that the world has ever seen. That opportunity was sacrificed to the interests of international finance. More and more territory was sought for the purpose of gratifying the Jewish merchants: but no thought was given to the full development of natural resources for the benefit of the inhabitants.

For example, the Boer wars were not fought in order that every inch of South African territory might be made to yield up its store of natural wealth. They were fought in order that the Jews of Jo'burg[105] might gamble in gold and diamonds, at the expense of the agricultural population.

It may be taken as an absolute rule that throughout the vast extent of the Empire for many years, international finance has skimmed the profitable surface and spurned that honest wealth below, which means hard work rather than quick profits.

Truly the City of London has created an Empire of Jewels in which men die for lack of bread.

And mark you, when the hungry complain, they are given, just like the hungry at home; not bread but democratic principles.

Just as Liberal Capitalism encouraged the ideology of democracy in England, so it has done in the Empire, with the result that many poor, simple peoples have been led to believe that if they only get Parliaments as good as that at Westminster, their troubles will be over. Poor, innocent creatures! It is impossible to lay too much emphasis on the fact that most of the so-called democratic movements in the Empire are welcomed by the international financiers, and for these reasons:

1. These financiers hate political coordination in reality. They prefer to weaken the bonds of authority, lest authority should demand justice.

2. They are interested not in political development but in economic exploitation.

3. When "nationalist" movements resort to force, the excuse arises to use military measures for which there would be no pretext otherwise. These measures can generally achieve a certain economic object much more quickly than patient negotiation or good government.

4. If the nationalism of the Imperial peoples can be safely diverted into the channel of democracy, it will be as harmless to international finance as every democratic system must necessarily be.

In India, for example, the nationalist movements have received encouragement from many English politicians: and, in theory at any rate, many concessions have been made to the idea of democratic autonomy: but I do not know of one prominent English politician who

[105] A reference to the large Jewish population of Johannesburg, South Africa, known as the "Randlords" who owned the goldmines and other mineral wealth of that country.

has proclaimed the necessity for a financial revolution as a necessary preliminary to the solution of India's problems.

So long as Indians are kept talking about representation, councils, responsibility, federation, democratic machinery and all the rest of the democratic Mumbo-Jumbo emanating from Westminster, so long will all their agitation fail to bear on the real troubles of their land.

The same is true, in principle, of Scottish Nationalism. There are honourable exceptions: but most of the Scottish Nationalists seem to think that their battle will be won when Scotland has a Parliament of her own.

They might have made more progress had they not laid emphasis on their desire to create at Edinburgh something as revolting to common sense as the assembly that sleeps at Westminster.

When they talk quite worthily of the national aspirations of the Scots, they usually omit to say what they propose to do with the Royal Bank of Scotland, which has so many intimate associations with international finance.

A healthy feeling of Nationalism is both natural and desirable; but it is hard to resist the impression that the Jewish Lords of Finance are seeking to exploit this feeling in certain places, in order to distract attention from the need for economic revolution.

History has shown that, in certain circumstances, it is quite possible for different races to belong in concord to a common system and to accept discipline under it. Such a condition may, in time, develop into an integral unit and the world profit thereby: but this conception of Empire demands both economic justice and economic progress. If neither exists, complaints are bound to arise: and, when they do arise, it is much easier for the architects of evil to talk about new experiments in government than to remedy the fundamental grievances by abandoning the system that causes them.

International finance is, unhappily, the master of the British Empire and has been for some years. The consequence is that whilst the financiers have reaped a rich harvest, the whole structure has been politically disintegrating for the last twenty years. As a general rule, conditions are worse in proportion to the power that Whitehall exercises in any particular part of the British Commonwealth of Nations. This fact is sad: but it must be faced.

The appalling conditions, for example, in Newfoundland are a most perfect argument for the concentration of Britain on her own affairs and for the abandonment of her pretence that she has a sacred mission to settle the affairs of Central Europe. One quarter of the population is starving, and tuberculosis stalks along with poverty as its faithful companion.

Whilst there can be little doubt that the greatest poverty in the Empire is found in India, it is hard, at present, to obtain exact information as to its extent.

With regard, however, to the so-called Colonial Empire, which is directly subordinate to Whitehall, no such difficulty arises. The truth can be read in the *First Report of the Committee on Nutrition in the Colonial Empire,* published in 1939 by His Majesty's Stationery Office. It consists of two volumes full of information: and merely to quote particular passages can give no adequate idea of the indictment against Democratic Imperialism which the whole embodies.

Amongst the Committee were Sir John Orr, Sir Edward Mellanby, Professor Cathcart, Professor N. F. Hall, and other famous scientists.

Although quotation is inadequate to convey the extent of the evil which exists, a few passages may be cited by way of example. The Committee states:

"The data available do not enable us to say with any accuracy, except where definite deficiency diseases are reported, that this or that deficiency exists in this or that territory: but we believe that almost everywhere health is impaired to a greater or less degree by malnutrition. We would go so far as to say that for every recorded case of a specific deficiency disease, there are hundreds of cases of absence of full health due in part at least to malnutrition."

The first general conclusion of the investigators is this:

"To sum up, Colonial diets are very often far below what is necessary for optimum nutrition. This must result not only in the prevalence of specific deficiency diseases but in a great deal of ill-health, lowered resistance to other diseases, and in a general impairment of well-being and efficiency. There is in our minds no doubt whatever that these conclusions are correct."

Then the Committee deals with the causes of this scandal:

"The main causes of malnutrition in the Colonial Empire are in our view, first, that the standard of living is often too low: and secondly that there exists widespread ignorance . . . a low standard of living and ignorance react to some extent on one another. If there were greater wealth in the Colonial Empire, Governments could spend more money on removing the ignorance, and if there were less ignorance, the available resources . . . would be used to greater advantage than they are at present."

It is all very well to picture a vicious circle of poverty and ignorance: but the Committee would have exceeded its terms of reference if it had dealt with the real problem-finance.

The most pertinent observation which can be made upon the whole problem is that six hundred million pounds have been lost by Britain in the countries of South America; of course, much of the investment in these countries has brought high dividends to the investors. But every single penny placed in the Crown Colonies has been begrudged.

We must repeat that the International Financier would far sooner risk his money in the hope of high profits than invest it for a relatively low return in the development of lands where hard and patient work is needed before any considerable profit can be reaped.

Of course, there is no difficulty in finding "capital" to finance the production of useless precious stones or an easily won commodity like sugar. There is always an abundance of the cheapest labour available. But the scientific and conscientious development of the agricultural resources of this vast Empire would be deemed a bad business proposition by the Jewish Imperialists of the City. They want the cream: the microbes can have the skim.

The report provides some illuminating comment on Colonial wages. One passage runs:

"It would probably be easy to compute that the wages paid—say 10 s. a month in East Africa, 15 s. a month in West Africa or 1 s. to 1 s. 3 d. per day in the West Indies—are not sufficient to provide a man and his family with the food that they ought to have . . . For instance, it has been calculated that the minimum sum required to obtain a reasonably good diet (not an optimum diet) in Freetown (Sierra Leone) is between 6 d. and 7 d. per head per day, or say 15 s. per month. That is just about, the average wage received by the urban labourer, so that, according to this computation, if he is to feed himself decently, there is nothing left at all for the food of his wife and family, let alone for his housing, clothing, etc., unless he has other sources of income."

Yet, in the face of these figures, British politicians dare to talk about oppressed Czechs and Poles.

They conveniently forget that in their Colonial Empire the rate of infant mortality lies between 10 per cent and 40 per cent of all the children born. Even more presumptuous is the thesis advanced at Westminster that Germany is not qualified to possess or administrate colonies. Whatever her failings might conceivably be in this respect, even if she deliberately tried to ruin her colonies, it is hard to see that she could do worse than successive British Governments have managed to accomplish.

In Cyprus, for example, "a considerable number of the rural population are, on account of poverty, definitely underfed and thus liable to tuberculosis, colds, infectious diseases, and epidemic ophthalmia, the incidence of all of which is high, especially among the underfed."

Since 1931, the Cypriots have been forced to accept British rule by military measures: tens of thousands of peasants are homeless: and the taxation imposed upon the people has been intolerably oppressive.

Yet, if Germany had said: "We don't like the way you are handling weaker people of a different race," and declared war on Britain in the interests of small peoples who wanted to be free from her, the British politicians would have been very surprised indeed, as would the whole British people. Yet, she would have had an incomparably better case than Mr. Chamberlain had on September 3, 1939.

In this chapter, every effort is being made to avoid both recriminations and the Tu Quoque style of argument.[106] But it is impossible to ignore facts.

It is not necessary to recite a list of crimes committed by Britain to establish the fact that her Empire depends on the use or principle of force. Every sensible human being knows that force may be either rightfully or wrongly applied: and there is no intention here of conducting a series of ethical inquiries.

It is a fact that the South African Dutch would declare a Republic tomorrow, if the threat of British force did not prevent them from so doing. The same is true of Eire.

The present century has seen the use of armed force against both the South African Dutch and the majority of the Irish people. Rhetorical embellishments are not needed to describe either case.

If England claims that she had good reasons for acting as she did, Germany can claim to have had better reasons for moving to protect her own flesh and blood in Poland or other areas torn away from her by

---

[106] The appeal to hypocrisy is an informal logical fallacy that intends to discredit the opponent's position by asserting the opponent's failure to act consistently in accordance with that position.

force. In both South Africa and Ireland, the history of England's failure has been tragic. In the former, the Jewish trader in gold and diamonds was granted a monopoly of the Union Jack, with the result that the Boer farmers felt themselves compelled to fight for their lives against an Oriental despotism.

If one sixth of the money invested and lost outside the Empire, in South America alone for example, had been given to Ireland, there might have continued that cooperation between her and England which provided British history with Burke, Goldsmith, Sheridan, Wellington, Boyle, Roberts, French, Beatty and Carson.

As though, however, by an inevitable destiny, International Finance wound its coils round the heart of England, and its venom was carried throughout the bloodstream to the whole Colonial and Imperial system.

Today, India is in a ferment. Nowhere has it been more fashionable than in England to talk about the necessity of democratic self-government for India. Here I express a purely personal opinion, which is intended to commit nobody else. If democracy has proved such a curse to Europe, there can be no justification for inflicting it upon the unsuspecting Indians.

In fact, they have no political unity: the Princes, the Moslems, and the Hindus of British India are not likely to agree. In my own opinion, autocracy in some form or other is the natural lot of the Indian peoples for generations to come: and it is a form of Government which they understand and respect when honestly administered.

India's most urgent troubles are economic. Her cotton-mills have been used to grind out of her slave labour cheap goods which have destroyed Lancashire. Nowhere has any attempt been made by the Government to bring about that financial revolution which is fundamental to Indian well-being.

Until the people are freed from the grip of the bunya, or moneylender, they will be miserable. Moreover, the soil could be made to yield up the needs of the people, but only by a dictatorship strong enough to override all private interests, strong enough to base the whole financial system on the realities of production and consumption.

No doubt, Indian readers will be disappointed if I write in this strain: but in objective argument, it is necessary to remember that British irrigation has saved the lives of millions and that, in the old days, at least, British administration won a respect which it deserved.

With the onset, of course, of the Sassoons and their friends against the Indian urban population, the issue became confused. Moreover, Britain could have done infinitely more than she did: but credit must be given where credit is due. It was not the British administrators, but the financiers behind British Governments that brought about the present situation.

The tariffs against British cotton goods and British steel were imposed by arrangement between the Schusters and their fellow Jews, not to protect the Indian worker with his bowl of rice, but to protect the vested interests of international Jewish finance at the expense of England herself.

India was mapped out as a special field for Jewish exploitation, partly because of her natural wealth, and partly because of the disgraceful cheapness with which labour could be obtained.

It was Montague, a Jew, who began to stir the Indian peoples out of "their pathetic contentment": it was Rufus Isaacs, or Lord Reading, who pursued this policy.

These gentlemen were afraid that the conscience even of a British Parliament might revolt against the labour conditions which capitalism in India had brought into being. The solution was, then, some Government less closely connected with Westminster: for the Jews had and have the supreme confidence that they could bribe any Indian Government into amenability.

Despite the reforms which have taken place, Indian finances are still controlled by the Schuster school: and whatever proposals were made by British democrats for the granting of autonomy to India, it was always understood that the Army should remain there to make sure that capitalist interests should be protected.

Nobody acquainted with India supposes that the peace would last long if the Army were withdrawn. Nevertheless, it would be wrong to suppose that it is there for the sole purpose of preventing the Indians from quarrelling amongst themselves.

The Indian nationalist is apt to blame England for everything: if he would only look behind the facade which the word England represents, he would see that he and the English themselves are the victims of the same evil forces.

If the British Empire today is merely a conventional phrase, it is Britain's politicians who are to blame: and the fault did not begin with this generation. No true Imperialism is compatible with the principles of International Finance. That is why the Jew Einstein agreed to become President of the League Against Imperialism.[107] As the head of a society pledged to smash up the British Empire, he was naturally, when he visited England, accorded the honours due to royalty: and that libidinous little nincompoop, Oliver Locker-Lampson, mounted guard over him with a shot-gun, lest any wicked Nazi should attempt to injure him. Photographs were published in the Press, showing the exponent of relativity and his bodyguard.

Yet nobody had paid more lip-service to the Empire than this Sancho Panza with his shot-gun. This instance reveals very typically the antagonism between Jewry and real Imperialism. Naturally, a real empire would aim at and probably achieve autarchy—or self-sufficiency. At any rate, such an achievement would not have been beyond the British Empire, had it possessed any real unity.

It was largely because England refused to treat her Dominions and Colonies any better than foreign nations that she lost their confidence. Even as early as the eighteenth century, the attempt to treat colonies as a mere source of profit was in large measure responsible for the American Revolution.

Until 1933, then, the Jews hated the idea of the British Empire. In practice, as distinct from theory, they tolerated and controlled it as a means of spreading the ramifications of their finance more widely. But any suggestion that the Empire should acquire the psychological basis of unity, and any suggestion that the countries of the Empire should form an economic unit was regarded by international finance as a menace.

To say that all Jews adopted this attitude would be an exaggeration: but as a body, they have never had more than two uses for the British Empire. The first, prior to 1933 was the use of political power on behalf of their own financial interests.

The second, since 1933, has been the use of this loose but potentially wealthy conglomeration of states, half-states, principalities and what not against National-Socialist Germany. In plain language, it was not the post-war intention of Jewish finance that the Empire should exist in any but a financial sense: but on the day when Adolf Hitler became

---

[107] The League against Imperialism was founded in the Egmont Palace in Brussels, Belgium, on February 10, 1927, in presence of 175 delegates, among which 107 came from 37 countries under colonial rule. The Congress aimed at creating a "mass anti-imperialist movement" at a world scale, and was a front organization of the Communist International, the Comintern. Albert Einstein would later resign from the presidency of this organization because it opposed the Zionist colonization of Palestine.

Reichskanzler of Germany, all their plans were reversed. Examine every weakening of Imperial ties between 1919 and 1933. A Jew will be found lurking somewhere in the background, whether it be Otto Kahn, Rufus Isaacs, Montague or Samuel, Schuster or Hamar Greenwood.

Examine every exhibition of Imperial flag-wagging since 1933, and a chorus of Jews will be observed dancing in the foreground. Thus the whole idea of that beneficial political integration, so helpful to progress has been lost from the British Empire, and the currents of Empire-building turned awry.

Perhaps, there is no more shameful example of Jewish influence on British politics then the policy which England has been pursuing in Palestine for the last two years. Both Arabs and Jews were promised paramountcy in the same region during the war.

The Arabs got the promise first: but Chaim Weizmann's power over Balfour[108] was such that he was soon able to extract from the British Government an undertaking diametrically opposed to the pledge that was given to the Arabs.

Nobody was more disgusted with the treatment meted out to the latter than T.E. Lawrence,[109] who was mainly responsible for their having supported Britain during the war. In fact, of the many great servants of Britain who have been disillusioned, none was ever more disgusted than he. He did not live to see the full consequences of the betrayal.

During the last two years, the Arab majority in the country of Palestine has been taught the meaning of democracy, by a campaign of murder, torture, and arson carried out, most unfortunately, by the armed forces of the British Crown, both Jewish and Aryan. Needless to say, the civilian Jews have lent a hand in the good work.

---

[108] Arthur James Balfour, (1848–1930) was a British Conservative politician who was the Prime Minister of the United Kingdom from July 1902 to December 1905. In 1917, while serving as Foreign Secretary, he issued the famous "Balfour Declaration" which took the form of a letter addressed to Baron Rothschild (Walter Rothschild, 2nd Baron Rothschild), a leader of the British Jewish community, for transmission to the Zionist Federation of Great Britain and Ireland, in which it was stated that the British government was in favor of establishing in Palestine a "national home for the Jewish people."

[109] Thomas Edward Lawrence (1888–1935), an archaeologist and British Army officer renowned especially for his liaison role during the Sinai and Palestine Campaign, and the Arab Revolt against Ottoman Turkish rule of 1916–18. Better known as Lawrence of Arabia, he died in a suspicious motor cycle accident, allegedly on his way to a Mosely meeting in 1935.

I am not judging by reports in either the German or the British press, still less by any partisan pamphlets which have been published, but, in the main, by the accounts which I have had from British officers who were present during the perpetration of these atrocities and powerless to avert them.

Officers who showed signs of an impartial attitude were very speedily removed from their command. One officer who, in a notorious case of homicide, insisted that disciplinary action should be taken against the servants of the Crown who were guilty of it, and shown to be guilty of it, was removed from his post and sent on long leave. He was given full pay, but kept away from Palestine. Further details of the case cannot here be given, lest his position should be further prejudiced.

How far all this oppression fits into the scheme of democracy was delicately suggested by the late Anthony Crossley[110] in the House of Commons on May 22, 1939. He said:

"I do not believe that there has ever been a debate in this House, when this House would have been more justified in calling to the Bar an Arab speaker to explain the Arab point of view from the viewpoint of his own countrymen and his own country . . . There are no Arab members of Parliament. There are no Arab constituents to bring influence to bear upon their members of Parliament. There is no Arab control of newspapers in this country. It is impossible almost to get a pro-Arab letter into the Times. There are in the City no Arab financial houses who control large amounts of finance. There is no Arab control of newspaper advertisements in this country. There are no Arab ex-Colonial Secretaries who one by one get up and thunder, as they will, at the Government during the debate, because of the mistakes they themselves have made in the past. Finally, and I want the Colonial Secretary to pay special attention to this point, tomorrow night there is to be a broadcast. There is to be himself giving the Government point of view. There is to be the honourable member for the Don Valley to advance what is obviously the Zionist point of view. There is to be the honourable member for Carnarvon Boroughs supporting the Zionist point of view. There will not be a supporter of the Arabs who can advance their point of view."

The above passage is worth reading again and again. Mr. Crossley did not observe that there was also no Arab Secretary of State for War

---

[110] Anthony Crommelin Crossley (1903–1939) was a British a writer, publisher and Conservative politician. He died aged 36, when the aircraft in which was travelling crashed into the sea off the Danish coast on 15 August 1939.

to give instructions to the troops in Palestine: but he went as near as he dared to delineating the Jewish control of Britain. At any rate, his analysis is a striking commentary on the freedom of speech which democracy permits.

Now let us see what the Chosen People were saying. There was neither reserve nor delicacy in their remarks. The *Daily Herald* of July 17, 1939, contains this report:

"An appeal to the British people over the heads of the Government is to be made by Jews. This was decided on at an emergency meeting of the Zionist Federation of Great Britain and Ireland ... Several hundred delegates, summoned by telegram from all parts of the country, attended the meeting. The Chairman, the Rev. M. Perlzweig, said the Jewish people were in conflict not with the British people but with the British Government ... Professor Brodetsky, head of the political department of the Zionist organization, said the terrorized Jews of Europe had either to accept this decree of death or defy it and live. They would do everything in their power to make the Government's policy impossible to carry out."

The "decree of death" was the Government's open proposal for compromise between Jews and Arabs. Some sort of gesture had to be made in a desperate attempt to save the face of democracy: but of course the Government could not be expected to stand up to the threats of Professor Brodetsky.[111]

Every such speech as he made was the signal for a renewed outburst of violence against the Arabs in Palestine: and just to show that Jewry was in earnest, some of the confraternity in Palestine shot British soldiers and police—only, of course, those who were not hostile to the Arabs.

It may be recollected with some humour that Mr. Malcolm Mac Donald[112] increased the proportion of Jews in the Palestine Police with a view to facilitating the restoration of order.

Chaim Weizmann was a little more polite than Brodetsky. He said, on May 18, at the Kingsway Hall:

[111] Selig Brodetsky (1888–1954), a Russian-born Jew who served as a member of the World Zionist Executive, the president of the Board of Deputies of British Jews, and the second president of the Hebrew University of Jerusalem.
[112] Malcolm John MacDonald (1901–1981), appointed in 1938 to the office of Dominions Secretary and to oversee the Colonial Office. In 1939 MacDonald oversaw and introduced the so-called MacDonald White Paper which aimed at the creation of a unified state. The White Paper argued that with over 450,000 Jews having now settled in the mandate, the Balfour Declaration had now been met.

"Far be it from me to use language which suggests a threat, but it is my duty to utter a warning against the inevitable effects of this policy."

The warning, of course, took effect: and the lot of the Arabs became harder than ever. The Government, with Hore-Belisha grinning all the time, had made that feeble little gesture of affected impartiality which the Public School tradition demands: it had been misunderstood: and accordingly there was nothing for it but to defer to the wishes of Sir Samuel Hoare's favourite people.

Space does not permit us to give details here of the hard lot that the Arabs have had to endure. But anybody who wants to know the truth will at least take the trouble to consult some representative Arab from Palestine as well as his Jewish opponent. Unless the reader is prepared to take this step, he should refrain from assuming that the Arabs have no cause for discontent.

The killing and maiming of Palestine Arabs, the starvation in the Colonial Empire, the sweating of slave labour in India, the growing unrest in Ireland, the resolve of the South African Dutch to cut adrift from England may or may not form sufficient material on which to conduct a case against the British Empire as it is now being and has for some time been conducted: but these facts do undoubtedly stop the politicians of Britain from declaring with a single shred of conviction that Germany is not qualified to possess a Colonial Empire.

The agents of the Third Reich would have to be much more depraved than they are pictured by the Left Book Club[113] before they could rival some of the more recent performances of British agents in Palestine.

The claim that native populations must not be transferred to German control overlooks the fact that they were torn away from Germany without any pretence at consultation. Germany has never asked for one quarter of the world: Britain apparently does not think this modest fraction enough.

Germany has not asked for a tenth or for a twentieth of the earth, although her population is nearly twice that of Great Britain and likely to be more. Germany has asked only for that which was developed, formed, fashioned, and made productive by the honest sweat of

---

[113] The Left Book Club was a publishing group that exerted a strong socialist influence in the United Kingdom from 1936 to 1948, and is credited with helping the Labour Party to win its landslide victory of 1945. Pioneered by the Russian-born Jew Victor Gollancz, it issued a monthly book choice, restricted to members only, as well as a newsletter that acquired the status of a major political magazine. It also held an annual rally.

German workers and pioneers, who have no reason to regard Britain's Empire-builders as their superiors.

Again the Führer declared most solemnly that such Colonial differences as existed between Germany and Britain should never be regarded as forming a *Casus Belli*. What colonies Germany had before the last war were won peacefully by hard work.

Germany is not seeking a vast expanse of territory over which international financiers can play their game of speculation with diamonds and gold, whilst real wealth lies untapped and scorned. She wants merely that for which her sons and daughters have worked, in order that she may play her due part in the age-long struggle of man to wrest his needs from nature.

Every inch of ground that Germany has at home and abroad, each single inch, is and will be consecrated to the purpose of enabling ordinary people to live a fuller, happier, and more prosperous existence.

If this aim is contrasted with the almost inscrutable stimuli which agitate the British Empire and keep it in sickly being, there can be no doubt as to the course which the dynamic development of history will take.

Chapter VIII: British Foreign Policy and the Ultimate Causes of this War

THE purpose of this chapter is to attempt an elucidation of the issues at stake in this present struggle. It is not proposed to make a detailed examination of the immediate causes which led to Mr. Chamberlain's declaration of war on September 3, 4939. Such an analysis exists in the most perfect form attainable in the *German White Book* on the origins of the war. This remarkable collection of documentary evidence deserves to be read as a whole: and only when it is considered as a whole, can the full strength of the indictment which it embodies be appreciated.

Neither is it possible to recount in detail or even in outline the course of that jagged and vacillating Foreign Policy which Britain has pursued since 1918. A contribution, however, to this subject which no student of international relations can afford to miss is John Scanlon's *Very Foreign Affairs*.[114] It is a volume full of interesting quotations, of which two only are here cited as specimens. He quotes Ramsay Mac Donald as saying:

"Were I a German Minister and had the responsibility of deciding whether I should or should not sign (the Treaty of Versailles), I should do the former only after making it plain that my signature was obtained under compulsion, and that the provisions were such that I could not guarantee that they would be carried out."

He also at Leeds on October 49, 1919, asked his hearers "to put themselves in Germany's position of having done their best to carry out the Peace Treaty and having found that, instead of the punishment coming steadily towards an end, it was becoming heavier. What would they do? They would repudiate that Treaty as soon as they got a chance."

On which Mr. Scanlon comments "Herr Hitler was being justified in advance."

In England, after the last war, there was a wide diversity of opinion as to what should be done with Germany: but there was a general

---

[114] *Very Foreign Affairs*, John Scanlon. Allen & Unwin (1938).

conviction that the Kaiser and his people had caused the war and must pay a heavy price. The Kaiser was to be hanged by Mr. Lloyd George: but he solved the problem by going to live in a place where it would be impossible to hang him.

The German people could not follow his example: so they stayed at home and died by the hundred thousand of starvation, whilst the humanitarians of Versailles maintained the blockade against them for the whole of the winter after that fateful morning of November 11, when Germany laid down arms because the tentacles of Jewry had throttled her heart.[115]

British officers in the Rhineland wrote frantic protests home against the horrors of emaciation and inanition which they were compelled to witness. The only answer to their protest was the gesture of the ever chivalrous French in sending black troops to the German cities to bully the men and molest the women.[116]

And then some people wonder why Germany grew tired of the Treaty of Versailles! Nothing could seem worse to the German than to think of his womenfolk at the mercy of these black brutes: but this was not the end of the price that Germany was to pay for a war that Jacob Schiff, of the firm of Kuhn Loeb in New York had sworn to bring about in order that he might avenge the deeds of Russia against the Jewish people.

Hardly had President Wilson finished his prayers for "joy in widest commonalty spread" than the Allies began the most idiotic and insensately cruel piece of buffoonery that the world had ever seen—the attempt to extract thousands of millions of pounds from the German people by way of "reparations." Of course, they could make the German workers toil for twelve, fourteen, or sixteen hours a day for practically nothing.

---

[115] The Blockade of Germany, started in 1914 and was a prolonged naval operation conducted by the Allied Powers to restrict the maritime supply of raw materials and foodstuffs to Germany. The German Board of Public Health in December 1918 claimed that 763,000 German civilians died from starvation and disease caused by the blockade up until the end of December 1918. The blockade was maintained after the Armistice in November 1918, into the following year of 1919. The restrictions on food imports were finally lifted on 12 July 1919. At least a further 100,000 German civilians died due to the continuation blockade of Germany after the armistice.

[116] In 1919 France stationed between 25,000 and 40,000 black colonial soldiers in the Rhineland. The presence of such large numbers of Africans in such a small area led to an outbreak of crime and sexual offences against the white German women, and caused an uproar throughout Germany and in America.

They could arrange for the taxation of Germany till women and children cried in the streets for bread. The only thing they could not do was to confer any benefit upon their own peoples. When vindictive lunatics began seizing German railway-engines, the workers of Crewe[117] began to wonder why they were being paid off.

At the very time when the pundits of the Treasury Bench were moaning about dumping, they saw fit to institute the supreme form of dumping by confiscating German goods in kind, produced by the sweated and underpaid labour of German workmen, who saw their families without food whilst they worked day and night to cause unemployment in England.

When the long-eared incumbents of the Treasury Bench proposed that they should pay the U.S.A. in kind, they heard what can only be described in the most vulgar language as a "mouthful."

The business acumen of the Yankees served as a warning to those who, in order to cut vainglorious capers at Election time, averred that Germany must pay the last mark. Still, year after year, the persecution went on.

The Germans had no doubt that they were in the right in fighting England after she had declared war on them in 1914. I have never yet met one English patriot who could tell me why the last war was fought. Until 1933, all the Socialists were of opinion that it had been fought in the interests of Capitalism.

To ascertain its real causes, one would have to go intimately into the details of the intrigues of Edward VII, the Speyers, the Cassells, the Ballins, the Battenbergs, and all those highly placed personages who saw some virtue in bringing Germany and England to grips in 1914.

But the best commentary on the whole thing is given by Alec Waugh,[118] who describes a British soldier standing on an English station platform in the early days of the war, brandishing his rifle, and triumphantly exclaiming: "Wait till I get at those bloody Belgians and I'll show 'em."

There could be no greater condemnation of British democracy than that such a war should have been waged without any knowledge on the part of the British public as to the causes. And the ordinary man in England had no more interest in France and Belgium than in the correct reading of disputed lines in *Beowulf.*

---

[117] A (former) train manufacturing hub in the northwest of England.

[118] Alexander Raban "Alec" Waugh (1898–1981), a British novelist, the elder brother of the better-known Evelyn Waugh.

Perhaps the funniest instance of the attitude adopted by some people lies in the work of Dr. G.P. Gooch, the fifth-rate historian, who wrote some ten volumes before 1933 designed to show that Germany was not guilty of having brought about the last war. But after Hitler's accession to power, two further volumes were added to show that Germany had been responsible after all.

At any rate, Germany sank deeper every day into the slough of social democracy. As Jewish corruption entwined itself about her limbs, as she became the tool of International Finance, she found plenty of friends. When starvation had broken her spirit of independence, when the benevolent dispensers of Versailles had satisfied themselves that she would work obediently as a member of the international conspiracy, she was once again invited to enter the thieves kitchen.

Bishops and Archbishops arose in the pulpit and demanded her admission into the League of Nations. Nothing, of course, was done to help the German people. They still had to bear their intolerable burden: but the growing Jewish capitalist class in Germany had as much right to a place at the Council Board as their compeers from London and Paris.

The oily Hebrews who had made fortunes during the inflationary period could not possibly be kept out of the comity of nations. Their tools and dupes, like Streseman[119] and Brüning[120] were unanimously voted "good fellows," whilst the German working man lay bruised and bleeding, "none so poor to do him reverence."

In those days, the chief danger of Nationalism seemed to come from Mussolini, who was accordingly belaboured with all the abuse that the journalistic hacks could excogitate. He was the "mad-dog" of Europe. He was always being threatened and never touched. The Jews believed

---

[119] Gustav Stresemann (1878–1929), a German politician who served as Chancellor in 1923 and Foreign Minister from 1923–1929, during the Weimar Republic. During his political career, he represented three successive liberal parties; he was the dominant figure of the German People's Party during the Weimar Republic.

[120] Heinrich Brüning (1885–1970) was Chancellor of Germany during the Weimar Republic from 1930 to 1932. He established a "presidential government," basing his administration's authority on presidential emergency decrees which were instituted without prior consent of the Reichstag. After Hitler became chancellor in January 1933, Brüning campaigned against the new government in the March 1933 elections, but was defeated. Later he yielded to his party's executive decision to dissolve itself, and left Germany in 1934 via the Netherlands and settled first in the United Kingdom, and in 1935 in the United States. In 1939 he became a professor of political science at Harvard University, remaining a life-long opponent of Hitler and National Socialism.

that he could be killed with bluff and ridicule: and, at that time, his policy was not openly anti-Jewish.

People in England who subsequently came to admire Fascism said rude things about him: but nobody seriously visualized Italy as a military rival of Great Britain's. Indeed, sometimes, when England grew jealous of France, as she often did, this ferocious madman, with his bludgeons and his castor-oil, suddenly became a refined and almost Christian gentleman, who had done so much for his people, who were in any case hardly human, that one must treat him with respect and say a few kind words about Garibaldi and Dante Alighieri.

The Duce has a keen sense of humour, and he must have laughed for many hours at the curious metamorphoses through which he was made to pass. Once, indeed, when the *Jewish Chronicle* was more than ordinarily angry with Hitler, it described Benito Mussolini as a "more enlightened type of Fascist."

Whatever he thought about these curious fluctuations in his popularity, he went on steadily improving the lot of the Italian people and arming them to meet the contingencies ahead.

Meanwhile the League of Nations, about which we have said nothing yet, was dribbling and drooling on, taking each opportunity of demonstrating its own impotence. It was founded ostensibly to serve as a court of international diplomacy, primarily to enforce the Dictate of Versailles, and fundamentally as the chief agency in Europe for the transaction of business concerning Jewish power politics.

From the start, it was a failure. Woodrow Wilson, who founded the thing, could not persuade his own people to have anything to do with it. Indeed, when he explained what he had done to Europe, grave doubts arose as to his state of mind. However, the Yankees cared very little what happened to Europe: and they shrewdly thought that if Woodrow had fooled them, well—the joke was on them.

Actually, the Secretariat of 600 Jews who swooped down on Versailles had more serious ideas.

They were not displeased at all with the flaccid character of the League. The longer the *Goys*[121] could be kept talking nonsense, the easier it would be to pick their pockets.

At any rate, Geneva would provide a marvellous centre for the weakening propaganda of internationalism. The Hebrew humorist

---

[121] Short for *Goyim*, the derogatory Yiddish word for Gentiles, originally meaning cattle, or sheep.

found something excruciatingly funny in the idea that difficult internal problems of the British Empire should be handed over to Señor Bustamente[122] of Cuba for solution.

It was a rare old treat to see the representative of Timbuctoo[123] getting up and putting France in her place.

And the deadly gravity with which the Germans treated the whole solemn farce was perhaps the most amusing item in the programme.

Just as in Freudian psychology, Jazz, and Surrealism, the Jew loves to see the poor *Goy* making a thorough ass of himself, crawling downstairs on all fours as it were, with top-hat on head and a piece of soap in his mouth, so there was something delightful to the Jewish mind in all the gabble that went on, all the mummery, and the thousand possibilities of shady intrigue that arose every day.

The League was to prevent war. When it tried to prevent war between Bolivia and Paraguay, it was told to mind its own business.

When it tried to prevent war between Japan and China, it was told to mind its honourable business.

When it tried to prevent war between Italy and Abyssinia, it was so thoroughly kicked in the guts that it died of peritonitis.

But the ghost twaddles on just as happily as ever. It has probably never noticed the dissolution, of its corporeal encasement. The almost unanimous condemnations by the League of Japan and Italy had no effect. Indeed the Hampstead Borough Council could have done far more to influence the situation than did the League. The Abyssinian war[124] marks a very interesting stage in modern European relations.

---

[122] Antonio Sánchez de Bustamante y Sirven (1865–1951) was a Cuban lawyer, professor of Public and Private International Law, Senator to the Cuban Congress, politician and two-time Judge of the Permanent Court of International Justice at the Hague (1922–1944).

[123] Timbuctoo is a real town in Mali, West Africa, quite deserving of its more popular use as an idiom in the English language as a place in the middle of nowhere.

[124] The Abyssinian War incident resulted from the ongoing conflict between the Kingdom of Italy (Regno d'Italia) and the Empire of Ethiopia (then commonly known as "Abyssinia" in Europe). The Italo–Ethiopian Treaty of 1928 stated that the border between Italian Somaliland and Ethiopia was twenty-one leagues parallel to the Benadir coast (approximately 73.5 miles). In 1930, Italy built a fort at the Walwal oasis. On November 22, 1934, a force of 1,000 Ethiopian militia with three Ethiopian military-political commanders arrived near Walwal and formally asked the garrison stationed there to withdraw from the area. Between 5 and 7 December, there was a skirmish between the garrison of Somalis, who were in Italian service, and a force of armed Ethiopians. Approximately 107 Ethiopians and 50 Italians and Somalis were killed. On October 3, 1935, shortly after the league exonerated both parties in

Mussolini, of course, was violently condemned in England. Nobody abused him more than Winston Churchill, who was so anxious to invoke the "traditional friendship" between England and Italy, when his country went to war with Germany. It seems doubtful, however, if England had any real intention of going to war over Abyssinia.

Nobody will ever know on what platform Mr. Baldwin fought the General Election of 1935. And for this reason, it is probably worthy to be described as the most brilliantly conducted Election of all time.

The Socialists, poor things, pretended to want the strongest "sanctions" against Italy, even if war should be the result: the "National Government" pretended to want the strongest sanctions against Italy, although hoping that war would not be the result but prepared to fight it if it came.

The National Government won, largely because its policy was harder to understand than the other: and because people could not understand it, they gave it the benefit of the doubt.

Of course, the truth of the matter is that although, in those days, Mussolini lost all his reputation for enlightenment, there had arisen in Germany a new movement and a man whose potentialities seemed so great that all available energies and resources had to be husbanded for the ultimate purpose of smashing him.

There was no telling what he might do, if Britain went to war with Italy: and he was the sworn enemy of Jewry. The starvation of the German people after the war, the mutilation of the Reich, the tearing away of its peoples and their subjugation to alien governments, the policing of the German cities with nigger troops, the frightful social conditions which existed on German soil, and the arrogance of the Jewish overlord very nearly cancelled the work of Friedrich Wilhelm the Great Elector, Frederick the Great, Stein, Scharnhorst, Bismarck, and Moltke.

That Germany was not hurled back into the chaos of 1648 and beyond, was the work of the man from the village of Braunau, born of poor parents, educated in hardship, and trained as a soldier in the trenches —shot at, first by the enemy, and then by his own countrymen—and chosen by God to take the world through the greatest revolution since

---

the Walwal incident, Italian armed forces from Eritrea invaded Ethiopia without a declaration of war, prompting Ethiopia to declare war on Italy, thus beginning the war. On October 7, the League of Nations declared Italy to be the aggressor. The war was over by May 1936, marked by a decisive Italian victory. The conflict became known as a symbol of League inability to achieve anything.

the Renaissance—Adolf Hitler. It was some time before the Sacred Geese[125] of Geneva started to cackle out the warning to their Jewish masters that Hitler was a dangerous man.

Thanks to the lead which the English took in propaganda, the Old School weapon of ridicule was used as the main method of stopping him. After the Munich Putsch, it was announced with joy that some presumptuous German nationalist had concluded a stormy little political career that never ought to have been begun.

Whilst the politicians of England were joking and sneering, Hitler was bringing the revolutionary creed of Nationalism combined with Socialism to Germany.

The cause had many martyrs. Jewish criminals paid liberally for the bloody corpse of every young Nazi that could be laid upon the mortuary slab. For a time, the little movement of patriotic Germans had to face contumely, violence, destitution, poverty, and death.

But Hitler had found the solution, and God gave him the courage and strength to persist in the face of every disappointment and every trial.

This man of whom the world had never heard wrote out his confession of faith in the fortress of Landsberg. He had found the solution. Where all the renowned thinkers of the age had failed, except, of course Mussolini, who was entirely concerned with the Italian people and their problems, he had seen the necessity for a synthesis of Socialism with Patriotism.

Patriotism was no longer to be the easy prerogative of the possessing classes: it was to be the common property of all: but it was to embody the ideal of economic revolution.

Socialism was purged of its class hatred and its denial of private property: nationalism was freed from the taint of snobbery: and the economic concept of National-Socialism received as its necessary background, the totalitarian theory already enunciated by Mussolini.

This new movement declared uncompromising war on Money-Power and Jewish Domination. The winning of the present war is a very light task in comparison with the winning of power in Germany.

Hitler was opposed by powerful enemies within and without. He was poor as poor could be in this world's goods. In the beginning, he had nothing but a tiny band of friends to serve as the material for victory.

[125] The Sacred Geese were, according to Livy, geese in the temple of Juno on the Capitoline Hill in Rome which saved the city from the Gauls around 390 BC when they were disturbed in a night attack.

The Party even had some difficulty in getting a typewriter. He had to convert a demoralized people. The massed forces of Jewry within and without were against him. The whole world was against him.

Day by day his strength grew: the tramp of his legions thundered through the streets of city, town, and village: the heroic strains of the Horst-Wessel song[126] arose in the later days as the challenge of a race reborn.

From 1928 onwards, every conceivable device was employed in the British Press to make Hitler appear ridiculous. I well remember a dinner that I attended early in 1932. It was a dinner of historians. There the celebrated Gooch assured his now frightened colleagues that Hitler would amount to nothing. A man who knew everything about Germany had told him so.

At this news, there was a great laugh, and calm descended on the port-bibbing assembly. I ventured to express precisely the opposite opinion and was stared at as if I were a hawker of ladies' underwear who had accidentally strayed into a monastery.

The Jewish publicist Laski, as late as 1932, wrote a newspaper article in which he jubilantly declared that Hitler had lost his chance. He had, it seems, faltered at the critical moment. He was unable to take decisions. Had he been a man of action, he would have marched on Berlin and shed all the blood that might be necessary to achieve his objects. No! It was clear beyond doubt that Hitler was not "one of us boys." He lacked the intelligence to take his chance when it came.

Beyond imagination therefore is the concert of Hebrew wailing which arose when this same Hitler became ReichsKanzler of Germany. The thing was inconceivable. The failure of "us boys" was beyond all comprehension.

However, hope springs eternal in the Jewish even as in the human breast. It was hoped at first that Hitler would become intoxicated with the sense of his own importance and thus fall an easy prey to the financiers, who well know how to flatter without losing their control.

So Hitler was represented as the tool of high finance. His manner of treating those capitalists who would not subordinate their interests to those of the state soon dispelled the illusion. Very soon the first legend

---

[126] The Horst-Wessel-Lied ("Horst Wessel Song"), also known by its opening words, *Die Fahne hoch* ("The Flag on High"), was the anthem of the Nazi Party from 1930 to 1945. The lyrics were written in 1929 by Horst Wessel, commander of the Storm Division (SA) in the Friedrichshain district of Berlin. Wessel was murdered by a Communist, and became a martyr for the entire movement.

was replaced by another: he was a Communist in disguise and was crushing the life out of private enterprise.

There is certainly no living man about whom more lies have been told: probably there are few in history.

Hitler soon began to do far worse things than had been expected. So long as the Storm Troops contented themselves with marching about and dealing with Jewish nuisances, the position was not so unbearably bad. After all, worse things were happening to the Jews in gallant little Poland every day.

The real enormity of his nature first became apparent when the unemployment figure of more than six million began to decline. Then everybody knew that the destinies of the Reich had passed into the hands of a dangerous madman. He was tampering with the economic system.

Worse still, even as the unemployment figure began to fall, production began to rise. In some industries it rose by 100 per cent: and after a few years, it had risen in certain cases by over 1000 per cent. As to this increase in commodities, the international financiers were not consulted at all.

Actually, the German currency was being cut adrift from their system: and in a little while, it became apparent that they would have no more to do with the economic structure of the New Germany than Dr. Crippen[127] with the curriculum at Eton.

The gloomiest fears had been realized. The Germans began to indulge in such depravities as the extraction of petroleum from coal and wood: they were caddish enough to devise a synthetic form of rubber: in fact, they were calmly lifting central Europe right out of the sphere of Jewish financial control.

Hitler had put into practice the awful theory that the worker is an integral part of the state and that the first function of government is to secure his interests. Some Germans of the old school were upset at the disappearance of their class privileges, and they found plenty of

---

[127] Hawley Harvey Crippen (1862–1910), usually known as Dr. Crippen, was an American homeopath, ear and eye specialist and medicine dispenser. After moving to London, he murdered his wife, for which he was later hanged. His case became famous because he was the first person to ever be arrested due to trans-Atlantic radio communication technology, then still in its infancy. Crippen had fled England in disguise on board a trans-Atlantic liner, but had been recognized by alert crew members, who used the ship's radio to alert the police back in London. Crippen was then arrested upon his arrival in Canada.

Englishmen and Judaeo-Englishmen to weep on their shoulders and console them.

The Jews left Germany in streams. Those who had opposed the national regeneration openly and actively were encouraged to leave. But the majority left because they saw that the possibilities of exploitation were gone and that England presented a much fairer field for their operations. I met one Jew who had left in the early days. He was treated in England as a martyr deserving of all the help and charity that could be bestowed on him. He was sent to a University and equipped free of cost for a professional life. He became a minor social lion as the victim of Hitler's tyranny. He knew my views well enough and therefore smiled quite cynically as he told me one December day that he was going back to Germany to spend the Christmas! On the other hand, the fact that so many Jews left of their own accord did not prevent them from doing their best to poison the minds of the British people against the Third Reich.

The measure of their sincerity can be judged by the fact that it became necessary for the Jewish Board of Deputies to issue a warning to Jews in Britain against instituting unfavourable comparisons between things in Germany and things in England.

Mussolini, too, was striving towards autarchy. Thus, if Austria and Czecho-Slovakia were brought into the National-Socialist system, the whole of Central Europe, from the Baltic to the Mediterranean, would have dropped out of the framework of the international-financial control. Right enough, the gaps began to fill up, and Jewry looked with horror upon the dissolution of its power.

Hitler had never made any secret of his intention to undo the Dictate of Versailles. Such was his supreme promise to his people. But his whole object was to redeem this promise in peace. The Saar was recovered peacefully. Austria realized that her destiny must be one with that of the Third-Reich.

Perhaps nothing in modern times is more comically pathetic than the enthusiasm with which Conservatives and Socialists alike in Britain hailed Dollfuss[128] as the model democrat. He is dead, of course: and by

---

128 Engelbert Dollfuss (1892–1934), an Austrian Christian Social and Patriotic Front statesman. Having served as Minister for Forests and Agriculture, he became Chancellor in 1932. In early 1933, he ordered the Austrian parliament dissolved and assumed dictatorial powers. Suppressing the Socialist movement in February 1934, he cemented the rule of "austrofascism" through the authoritarian First of May Constitution. Dollfuss was assassinated as part of a failed coup attempt in 1934.

virtue of the fact, he must have the sympathy of the British public: but, as a figure of history, he cannot claim the immunity from criticism due to a private person who has ceased to live.

He had two great claims to be regarded as the model democrat. First, as soon as he lost a majority in Parliament, he dismissed it and ruled by armed force. That he had no intention of holding an election was made abundantly clear to the Austrian National-Socialists, who represented the majority of the population.

Secondly, he showed no scruples about turning the guns on the Socialists of Vienna when they mistook democracy for social reform. By these two acts alone, Dollfuss climbed into the highest favour of all liberty-loving people in England. And it was clear to all that a hero had been found to champion liberty against the autocracy of Hitler.

Schuschnigg[129] was a worthy successor to Dollfuss. It seemed likely that, so long as he called no Parliament, he could enforce freedom in the manner approved by Lombard Street.[130]

In the end, however, the Austrian people grew tired of armed democracy and made it clear that the only alternative to bloodshed was the entry of Hitler's troops into the historic territory of the old German Empire. An election was at last held, much to the horror of every decent British democrat: and more than 90 per cent of the people voted for incorporation with the Reich to which by tradition, by language, and by race they belonged. Braunau[131] was now in Germany once more.

Only a few years before, Germany had been forbidden by France to make a Customs Agreement with Austria. Times had changed. There was much weeping and wailing amongst the elite in Britain over the *Anschluss*: but there was nothing to be done. The idea that the Austrians must be compelled to vote afresh, this time against Hitler, was a little too simple for the official mind.

Czecho-Slovakia was then taken up and used as a catspaw against Germany. There was always the hope that this anomalous creation of

---

[129] Kurt Alois Josef Johann Schuschnigg (1897–1977) became Chancellor of the Federal State of Austria, following the assassination of his predecessor in July 1934. After the absorption of Austria by the Third Reich—supported by the vast majority of the Austrian people—Schuschnigg was arrested and interned. In 1945, he left Austria for the United States where he worked as a professor of political science at Saint Louis University from 1948 to 1967.

[130] Lombard Street is a street in the City of London, notable for its connections with the City's merchant, banking and insurance industries, stretching back to medieval times. It has often been compared with Wall Street in New York City.

[131] Brannau-am-Inn, the Austro-German border town where Hitler was born.

Versailles might be used at a favourable moment for the overthrow of National-Socialism in Germany.

The treatment of the Sudeten Germans grew worse from day to day. They had been torn against their will from Germany by the victors of Versailles: they were treated as slaves by their Czech masters. The poverty in which they lived was appalling, and the conditions which they had to support were hardly fit for pigs, much less men and women. Again and again they had been promised redress of their grievances.

Indeed at the time when the forcible separation of Sudetenland from Germany occurred, they had been assured that the right of autonomy would be conferred upon them. Fifteen years went by without any attempt being made to redeem these promises. On the contrary, in 1938 they found themselves the victim of the merciless tyranny which Beneš,[132] on behalf of the Jews, was glad to exercise against a German people.

In their agony, they cried out for protection. England and France, still acting in defence of democracy, exerted every diplomatic effort to keep the Sudeten people under the military dictatorship of Prague. They failed.

Hitler was incapable of refusing to heed the call of his own blood. He made it plain that Sudetenland must come back to the Reich. In the days when the Jews wanted England to be weak, they had so thoroughly disarmed her that she had not had sufficient time to place herself in readiness for a first-class European war. Mr. Chamberlain therefore "compromised" at Munich—that is to say, he assented to the occupation of Sudetenland by German troops. He was far from claiming that he had given his assent under compulsion. Indeed, quite gratuitously, he asked for a mutual declaration signed by Hitler and himself to the effect that, in future, Britain and Germany would settle any differences between them by negotiation as opposed to armed force.

Although Mr. Chamberlain suggested this agreement and obtained it, he broke it without the least scruple on September 3, 1939, when he declared war on Germany, after having previously employed all the arts of delicate incitement to procure the general mobilization of the Polish Army. The ink on the declaration of Munich was scarcely dry, when the Jews, the City, and the Cabinet decided to scrap it. It would probably

---

[132] Edvard Beneš (1884–1948) was a leader of the Czechoslovak independence movement, Minister of Foreign Affairs and the second President of Czecho-Slovakia from 1935 to 1938 and again from 1940 to 1948 in exile.

be an injustice to say that Mr. Chamberlain was consciously insincere in the negotiations at Munich. He knew that England could not afford to go to war: but it is also quite probable that he himself would, at the moment, have preferred peace.

The crisis arose rapidly, the people of England wanted no war, no sensible Englishman wanted to die for Czecho-Slovakia, and there was no question of war between Britain and Germany, unless Britain made it. Anyhow, I have never seen such an ovation given to any human being as Chamberlain received when he returned to London with the Munich agreement in his pocket. The people were enraptured. Grown men and women were crying with joy.

As the Prime Minister drove through London from Hammersmith to Downing Street, the roaring of applause could be heard miles away from his route. Traffic was paralysed for hours: and in the dim light of the Churches, mothers and wives knelt down to pray in devout gratitude to their Maker that they had been spared the tragedy of another war. All reserve was abandoned. Complete strangers talked to one another like old friends, and it felt for a day as if the Kingdom of Heaven had come on earth. So much for the common people, the ordinary people—the people who would really have suffered if war came.

I hope that one day before his death Neville Chamberlain will realize the enormity of his crime in making the beauty of that experience a foolish myth of the irrecoverable past. He came nearer than any man to uniting England: but he lacked the element of greatness which would have caused him to prefer the heartfelt thanks of simple people to the approval of merchant princes and Jewish schemers.

The agents of International Darkness, the financiers, the Lords of Judah, the Satanists, the sons of Baphomet gnashed their teeth whilst the people cheered. To them it was gall and wormwood to see that English men and women cared nothing about Sudetenland or Czecho-Slovakia but solely wanted peace.

Still, they knew that if September the thirtieth belonged to the English people, October the first belonged to them—yes, and the days that followed. And, as the last sounds of celebration sank into the quietness of early morning, poor England's day was done.

The whole power of Judah and Freemasonry was mobilized rapidly: and in a few days, the Premier showed how the Munich Agreement was to be honoured by declaring that Britain must arm on an unprecedented scale. Minions of the Government like Earl de la

Warr[133] were prompted to say in public that Germany understood no argument but that of force.

Ironically enough, the solution of the Sudeten question was now being represented as the first real defeat that Hitler had suffered: as a bourgeois, Masonic doctor said to me: "Ha! Ha! Hitler has found somebody to stand up to him at last!" Yet a few days before, his wife had been weeping day and night at the thought of another war. So foolish are the English people!

Despite Britain's rapid armament for peace, Hitler still honoured the Naval Treaty, which kept the German Navy at one third the tonnage of the British fleet.

Each day, however, it became clearer that Czecho-Slovakia was being equipped as an arsenal for the destruction of the Third Reich. The only question was whether Germany should wait until all the plans for her elimination were complete.

Jewish criminals used Prague as a basis for their attempts to create internal dissension in Austria. Germans in Czecho-Slovakia were abominably treated: and, in the end, the Slovaks tired of the corrupt rule of Jewish warmongers, and, in the name of self-determination, appealed to Hitler to secure their autonomy against the military force of the Prague gangster.

Thus Czecho-Slovakia, the unnatural progeny of Versailles, came to an end. President Hacha[134] went to Berlin, and, without the use of any violence, the Bohemian-Moravian Protectorate was established, whilst Slovakia gained the independence which she sought.

These events have since been described repeatedly as Hitler's "great betrayal of Munich." But the British Government was fatally slow in formulating this charge: until the Jewish prompters came along with their indictment, the matter appeared in quite a different light to Mr. Chamberlain. There is one very definite reply to those who pretend that Britain was wrongfully treated in this crisis by Hitler. The *Evening Standard* of March 15, published the following statement:

---

[133] Herbrand Edward Dundonald Brassey Sackville, 9th Earl De La Warr, (1900–1976). The first hereditary peer to join the Labour Party and became a government minister at the age of 23. He was later one of the few Labour politicians to follow Ramsay Macdonald in the formation of the National Government and the National Labour Organisation. However, he ended his political career by serving as Postmaster General in the last Conservative administration of Winston Churchill.

[134] Emil Hácha (1872–1945) was a Czech lawyer, the third President of Czecho-Slovakia from 1938 to 1939. From March 1939, his country was under the control of the Germans and was known as the Protectorate of Bohemia and Moravia.

"'Britain is no Longer Bound by Czech Guarantee, says Premier...'
Britain no longer considers herself bound by the "moral obligation" to
consider her guarantee of the Czecho-Slovak frontiers already in force,
nor will the remainder of the 10,000,000 loan to Czecho-Slovakia be
paid at present. The Prime Minister made this statement in the House
of Commons today a few hours after the German troops had marched
into Prague. The statement was first made to the House of Lords by
Lord Halifax. The Foreign Secretary recalled that Sir Thomas Inskip,
some time ago, had told the House of Commons that, although the
formal treaty of guarantee had yet to be completed, the Government
felt under a moral obligation to treat it as being already in force. And
that in the event of unprovoked aggression against Czecho-Slovakia,
the Government would take all steps in their power to see that the
integrity of Czecho-Slovakia was preserved. Lord Halifax continued:
'Until recently the Government endeavoured to achieve an agreement
with the other powers represented at Munich on the scope and terms of
such a guarantee, but up to the present have been unable to reach any
such agreement. In the opinion of the Government the situation was
radically altered as soon as the Slovak Diet declared the independence
of Slovakia. The effect of this was to put an end by internal disruption
to the state whose frontiers we proposed to guarantee. Accordingly the
state of affairs described by Sir Thomas Inskip has now ceased to exist,
and H. M. Government cannot accordingly hold themselves any longer
bound by this obligation."

It would have been impossible to state more clearly and explicitly
the fact that Germany had not taken any action inconsistent with
Britain's obligations. If the whole situation was so altered by the internal
disruption of Czecho-Slovakia that the British Government could
no longer consider itself bound by its alleged obligation, under what
species of reasoning can it be supposed that Germany must remain
bound by a corresponding obligation, if any such thing existed? In
point of fact, the official statement made by Halifax acknowledges that
no contract had actually been made: it speaks of a "moral obligation,"
which was quite naturally dissolved when the artificial state concocted
at Versailles itself dissolved.

It is thus possible to dispose of the allegation that Hitler broke
faith by quoting the words of the British politicians themselves.
Nevertheless, within a few days' time, the Jewish machine was again
in full working order: and Mr. Chamberlain was denouncing Hitler's

"perfidy," although he well knew that the arguments advanced by Lord Halifax on March 15 were no less valid then than at the time when they were first stated.

If the situation had so changed that Britain was no longer bound by pledges and therefore was at liberty to abstain from any action, it must be inferred that there was no encroachment on her interests or undertakings. Consequently, Mr. Chamberlain's denunciation of Hitler was not only hypocritical but also impertinent.

What had at first appeared as a matter which did not concern Britain at all was transformed into the starting point of the last stage of the campaign for war. It was well known in Whitehall that the condition of the Germans in Poland was going from bad to worse: it was known that Danzig was being throttled to death by the Poles: and it was also understood that Hitler was determined to recover by negotiation the land which had belonged to Germany and the people who passionately wanted to be freed by their old Fatherland from the tyranny of Polish military dictatorship.

The Jews and their servants in Downing Street determined that Hitler should not succeed by negotiation. To prevent him from succeeding, two conditions appeared to be necessary. The first was that the Poles should be encouraged to reject every proposal made by Germany and to impress upon the Germans in Poland the absolute immutability of their lot: the second was that Russia should be engaged to do the main part of the fighting when the war broke out.

It is more than probable that Whitehall promised Russia as much of Poland as she wanted, provided that she would attack Germany. Anyhow, Lord Halifax was pleased to observe, after the Russian occupation of Poland, that there were two excuses: one that the bad example set by the Nazis had been followed: the other that, in any case, Lord Curzon had intended in 1918 that Russia should get just so much of Poland as she took for herself in 1939.

Whether it follows that Lord Curzon was a Nazi is a matter for expert logicians. But, at any rate, there could have been no harm in promising Russia what the good Lord Curzon had intended her to have.

On the other hand, the Old School tactic would probably be to suggest, by a series of winks and nods, that once Russian troops had occupied Polish soil for the purpose of attacking Germany and defending democracy, nobody could be so very unreasonable as to ask them to vacate the soil which they had fought to defend.

The Poles showed considerable uneasiness at the progress of the encirclement negotiations between Britain and Russia. What the Russians thought is sufficiently revealed by the ultimate outcome of the diplomatic campaign.

Stalin was not so simple as to mistake British suggestions for sound guarantees. Nor was he, it seems, very anxious to sacrifice Russian armies in a capitalist cause. His practical wisdom is shown by his having secured without a fight what Whitehall might have offered him for a million Russian lives. Outwardly, the policy of encirclement was going well. Inwardly it was crumbling. That the Russian Agreement with Germany came as a complete surprise to Mr. Chamberlain is too much to suppose. He knew that his masters wanted war and must have it. He was playing for high stakes. But the great purpose served by the Russian negotiations was to convince the British people, until the last moment, when all was over, that the Russians would enter the war against Germany.

When the news of the Russo-German pact broke upon London, the lesser politicians were paralysed. The Communists looked round thunder-struck, not knowing what to say. The *Daily Worker* appeared with a headline: "Stalin halts aggression in Eastern Europe."

Whereas Mr. Churchill had declared for months that without Russia all would be hopeless, whilst he had postulated as indispensable the alliance of those whom he had formerly called "Bloody Baboons," the whole press now set to work to prove that in some mysterious manner Stalin had cudgelled Hitler into submission. In the light of subsequent history, we can afford to smile at these speculations. As the final crisis approached, the Jewish propaganda engine, with its ten thousand-*Goypower* turbines, was churning out the material of hatred whereof war is made. To enumerate its bestialities would be as superfluous as it must be tedious.

One day Hitler was mad, the next day he was depressed, the next day dying, and finally it was shown that the real Hitler had been poisoned at Munich, not of course by Mr. Chamberlain, and replaced by twenty imitation Hitlers who had been assiduously coached for the job. Photographs were published showing the discrepancies between these impostors and the victim of Munich.

The imitation Hitlers were kept in a building: and Goring picked a few out for each day in accordance with the dramatic requirements of the situation for the time being.

Can one wonder that the British public should have been bemused when inundated with a hundred stories of this kind every week?

The films were enlisted to exhibit the dark deeds of Nazi spies made by the mile and cut off to the required length. A most hysterical Air Raid Precaution campaign was started. A poster was produced showing a comely young woman who needed protection. The Jews, however, soon noticed that she was blonde and accordingly had her removed and replaced by a dark lady whose portrait would have served equally well as an advertisement for the necessity of taking Beecham's pills.

Another picture showed a well-dressed man striding forward with a shield and looking with horror into the death-bearing skies. He seemed to be making the Masonic sign of distress.

The *Daily Express* was fairly frank. On July 21, 1939, it declared:

"And since Britain is the last refuge and strength of the Jews, the greatest service we can do to the Jewish race is to make this country an impregnable stronghold against aggression."

Thus were the people told for whom they must fight.

Concerning this avalanche of propaganda, an amusing story is told by the *Daily Express* of June 17. It runs:

"According to a reader, . . . an unfortunate ambiguity crept into a radio news talk the other day . . . Speaker was dealing with Nazi reactions to reports here of conditions in Germany. Nazis had described reports as 'baseless products of the new English lie-factory'—no doubt assuming he added without the glimmer of a smile in his voice, 'that the proposed Ministry of Information is already functioning.'"

Newspapers published serial stories describing how Nazis trampled women to death: and everything possible was done to make the British people hate Germany.

Except for the well-to-do and the parasitical classes, all this effort was far less productive than had been hoped. There was no popular movement for war: the masses of the people wanted peace: and therefore it became necessary to take sterner measures then mere propaganda could achieve.

Accordingly, with all pomp and panoply, a financial crisis was arranged. Mr. Chamberlain expected to go to the Country in the autumn, if peace survived so long. It was made perfectly clear to him that if peace did survive and he did go to the country, he would appear before the electors with a financial crisis in comparison with which that of 1931 would seem utterly insignificant.

When all else failed, the financiers started to drain their gold away from London. The City was rife with rumours of impending collapse. The *News Chronicle*, in its financial columns, blandly observed that foreigners had been selling sterling heavily, but that it must not be assumed that all foreign investments in Britain had been liquidated.

Such a moderate statement, tucked away in the decent obscurity of the financial columns, was calculated to cause more alarm amongst investors than glaring headlines announcing financial crisis. For the real financial crisis comes only when a few people think that they alone know what other people have also found out. They sell because they believe others to be ignorant of the prospective value of the shares.

Stockbrokers took the unprecedented step of cancelling their summer holidays. The pound began to slide. Hundreds of millions of pounds worth of gold were shipped to the U.S.A. And the stage was set for the prettiest financial panic that England had ever seen.

Mr. Chamberlain, as an orthodox financier of the old school had been set a problem which lay beyond his power to solve by any ordinary expedient or device. There was one way out—war! War would not only bring a transvaluation of all values: it would bring, for a time at least, the full support of Jewish Finance throughout the world.

In time of peace, the merchants would insist on their last shekel: for a Holy War against Germany, however, the Boys would club together as never before. Thus the Jews deliberately created a crisis which, if the whole system were to be preserved, they alone could solve.

Mr. Chamberlain's decision was taken in its most definite form within a few days after the August Bank Holiday. A Holy War was a much easier proposition than an election in the full blast of economic crisis. Now, it was only a question of time before the conflagration came.

The Polish Government, as a direct consequence of the unconditional pledges given by Mr. Chamberlain, was revelling in the persecution of its German subjects. As early as May, German men and women were hunted like wild beasts through the streets of Bromberg. When they were caught, they were mutilated and torn to pieces by the Polish mob, almost invariably led by Jews.[135]

When the streets of Bromberg were red with German flesh, Duff-Cooper[136] was boasting that Poland alone had the right to decide when

---

[135] *100 Documents on the Origin of the War,* German Foreign Office, Berlin. (German Information Office, New York, 1940).

[136] Alfred Duff Cooper, (1890–1954), known as Duff Cooper, was a Conservative Party

war should come. The little cissy whom Diana Manners[137] had adopted was highly jubilant at the thought that, technically at least, the privilege of starting the war should belong to Poland.

Nothing could more fully demonstrate the artificiality of the whole position than the fact that these warmongers pretended to be powerless to decide when or why England would have to fight. In any circumstances it would be difficult to believe anything so fantastic as this: but in view of Britain's failure to afford the Poles any military assistance whatsoever, except a few drums of poison-gas, there can be no doubt in the world but that Mr. Chamberlain knew when the war would come far more exactly than Beck[138] and Rydz-Śmigły.[139]

As the persecution of the Germans became intensified, Hitler pressed more vigorously for a decision. He knew well enough that if he waited long, there would be no Germans left in Poland to save. Every day the butchery increased: and thousands of Germans fled from their homes in Poland with nothing more than the clothes that they wore.

Moreover, there was no doubt that the Polish Army was making plans for the massacre of Danzig which never took place. The Polish Government was repeatedly promised the fullest military aid by Britain and France: it was urged, moreover, to concede nothing. The final German proposal that Danzig should be restored to the Reich and

---

politician appointed Financial Secretary to the War Office in 1931, Financial Secretary to the Treasury in 1934, War Secretary in 1935, and First Lord of the Admiralty in 1937. The most public critic of Neville Chamberlain's policy inside the Cabinet, he resigned in protest the day after the 1938 Munich Agreement. Cooper later took a prominent role in the famous Norway Debate of 1940, which led to Chamberlain's downfall, and became a target for German propaganda which presented him as one of Britain's three most dangerous Conservative warmongers. He later became the British Government's liaison to the "Free French" forces under De Gaulle (those Frenchmen who, in contradiction to the Geneva Treaty, took up arms once again after their nation had surrendered) in 1943. He subsequently became the British ambassador to France in 1944.

[137] Diana Cooper, Viscountess Norwich (née Lady Diana Manners; 1892–1986), a glamorous social figure in London and Paris.

[138] Józef Beck (1894–1944), Polish foreign minister in the 1930s, during which he was continuously involved in territorial disputes with Lithuania and Czecho-Slovakia. He left Poland after 1939, and died in Romania of tuberculosis.

[139] Marshal Edward Rydz-Śmigły (1886–1941) was a Polish politician, statesman, Marshal of Poland, and Commander-in-Chief of Poland's armed forces in 1939. In August 1939, he publicly declared Hitler an "enemy of the state" in a speech in Kraków. After Poland's defeat, he fled to Hungary, but returned to Warsaw in disguise in 1941 to help create a Polish underground, but died of heart failure two months after arriving back in Poland.

that the final destiny of the Corridor should be settled by plebiscite was scorned: indeed, the Poles would not even condescend to discuss it.

They were intoxicated by the promises of their gallant democratic allies who, in the sacred name of freedom, supported a military dictatorship of corrupt aristocrats against the right of an ancient German city to decide its own future. If they had not been such fools, they would have seen that this hypocritical attitude indicated an innate dishonesty of purpose incompatible with the idea of keeping faith.

But the Poles, with their natural weakness, showed all the savage joy of exultation at the prospect of trampling upon a superior people. They were even issuing maps showing all North Germany as far as the Elbe as their own territory. Polish generals talked of dictating peace on the Tempelhof in Berlin. Such was their temper that hostilities of some sort were inevitable.

On the nights of August 25th to August 31st inclusive, there occurred, besides innumerable attacks on civilians of German blood, 44 perfectly authenticated acts of armed violence against German official persons and property. These incidents took place either on the border or inside German territory. On the night of the 31st, a band of Polish desperadoes actually occupied the German Broadcasting Station at Gleiwitz.

Now it was clear that unless the German troops marched at once, not a man, woman, or child of German blood within the Polish territory could reasonably expect to avoid persecution and slaughter.

And the 44 attacks on Germany indicated the not remote possibility of an advance by the Polish Army of 2,000,000 on Berlin. It was all very well to argue that such an attempt was foredoomed to failure: but no General Staff has the right to make an assumption of this kind. Accordingly, the dawn of September 1 saw the armies of the Reich on the march.

In two days, Field-Marshal Rydz-Śmigły knew that all was lost and said so. But he was assured by the British Ambassador in Warsaw that the Siegfried Line had been broken in 17 places and that 1500 allied aeroplanes were on the way to Poland, laying Germany waste as they came. In the face of this overwhelming assurance, it would have been impolite to make peace whilst there was still a chance of saving something. After another two days, the chance had gone.

During the critical 48 hours which preceded 11 a.m. on September 3, 1939, not one of the people whom I met in Berlin could conceive that Britain would go to war with Germany. I told them that they were mistaken.

At twenty minutes past twelve Central European time, my landlady rushed into my room and told me: "Jetzt ist es Krieg mit England!" (It's war now, with England!) Her husband at once came in and shook hands with my wife and myself, saying: "Whatever happens, we remain friends."

We had known these simple people only since the previous day: they had no proof that I too was not an enemy: but their action was typical of the whole attitude of the German people.

At about 3 in the afternoon, the first newspapers announcing England's declaration of war were on the streets. They were given away free. Under the bridge outside the Friedrichstrasse Station, we all scrambled for papers. There was no sign of anger or hatred: people looked at each other as if the incredible had happened.

We went to tea with some friends whose name is famous in German history. They too felt no emotion except surprise and regret. We talked of England: and my host was so inspiring in his eloquence on the subject of what England might have achieved in friendship with Germany that, as I looked out on the twilight enshrouding the Kurfurstendamm,[140] I could think of nothing to say but Marlowe's famous lines:

"Cut is the branch that might have grown full strait
And burned is Apollo's laurel bough!"[141]

The Satanic nature of the conspiracy against National-Socialism transcended by far the particular occasion of the war. Anybody who could see clearly knew that this conspiracy was implacable.

For five years before any question of Austria, Czecho-Slovakia, or Poland arose, the British press and politicians had poured forth their incessant stream of hatred and abuse against the man who saved Germany. Every day, he was insulted in the Press to such an extent that only a man of exemplary patience would have consented to maintain diplomatic relations with the country that seemed bent on ruining him. When one looks back on the vile stories printed about the

---

[140] The Kurfürstendamm is one of the most famous avenues in Berlin. The street takes its name from the former Kurfürsten (prince-electors) of Brandenburg. This very broad, long boulevard can be considered the Champs-Élysées of Berlin.

[141] Scene XIV, from *The Tragical History of the Life and Death of Doctor Faustus*, commonly referred to simply as *Doctor Faustus*, a play by Christopher Marlowe, based on the German story Faust, in which a man sells his soul to the devil for power, experience, pleasure and knowledge. *Doctor Faustus* was first published in 1604.

Führer in the Ostrers' *Sunday Referee,* when one thinks of the slanders spoken against him from thousands of political platforms in England, when one remembers the lordly confidence of the Jews that National-Socialist Germany would be destroyed, the dramatic events of early September take their place in a perfect pattern.

Every apparently unrelated factor falls into its neat and proper series. The system of relations is complete, even down to the fact that Poland, who had in her time acted with some violence against the dynamic urge of the modern age, vanished from the map.

Hitler had dared to declare Germany independent of international finance. He had dared to find work for the unemployed. He had dared to claim that man should produce his maximum rather than cramp production to make profits for the few. He had dared to dethrone money as the god of the human race. He had dared to remove the class barriers thrown up on the pavement of gold. He had dared to invoke the Lords of Light against the powers of darkness.

And as the darkness receded from his German land, the hideous, grimacing monsters, the twisted evil spirits, the devils that spun the web of Perverse Fate, drew back muttering and snarling, foaming and cursing on the shadow's edge, and chanting with Satan:

"What though the field be lost,

All is not lost: the unconquerable will,

And study of revenge, immortal hate!"[142]

Whether that will to evil is unconquerable is the great issue to be decided finally in this war.

We have often heard before of revolts against particular nations: we have often heard of successful secession from some hated domination: but this is the first time in history that a rebellion on such a grand scale has arisen against the whole conception of international Mammonism.

For more than a century, the suffering of the poor, the proud man's contumely, the division of society into the fortunate few and the helpless many, the injustice implicit in Liberal Capitalism have called for a remedy and a remedy compatible with national traditions and knowledge of God.

When a man seeks to give this remedy, he must expect to have God with him and the Old World against him. So it is today.

---

[142] John Milton, *Paradise Lost.*

Chapter IX: The Present, the Future, and the Dynamics of the Age

IT would be premature to start writing a history of this war I when, at the time of writing, only five months of warfare have elapsed.

No such attempt will be made here. It will be enough to recount a few general impressions and then proceed to our analytical summary.

In England, the war began, typically enough, with a needless air raid alarm. For this reason, Mr. Chamberlain was half an hour late in making the speech that purported to explain why war had been declared on Germany.

Britain's conduct of hostilities showed that her Government had misjudged Germany in every particular. Whether Mr. Chamberlain and the thing that he picked up out of the political gutter to make First Lord of the Admiralty ever really intended to help Poland is a question open to doubt. It seems more likely that they regarded the Polish question as a useful pretext for a long-concerted plan.

In any case, the Polish War was over in 18 days: and had there been any disposition to save the "gallant ally," the chance was gone. Moreover, Russia, having carefully studied the advantages of an alliance with Britain and France, resumed the ownership of the territory that had formerly belonged to her. This was striking proof of the thesis so long advanced by the Left Book Club that Russia could do no wrong.

With Lord Halifax's lame apologies, we have already dealt. At first, the British warmongers pretended that they wanted to free the German people from their Government.

Between people and Führer, the most emphatic distinction was made. Months before, a brilliant English propagandist, Mr. Sidney Rodgerson had issued a solemn warning against this mistake. The German press and radio, instead of trying to suppress the argument that the German Leader and the German people were divided from each other, gave it the utmost publicity.

The result was that the German public at once identified this propaganda tactic of Britain's as a cheap attempt at disruption, based on complete ignorance of the situation. If anything had been required to give Germany greater unity in the hour of trial, here it was, presented on a silver plate.

When the mistake was tardily realized, Mr. Chamberlain was kind enough to include the German people in his condemnations and professions of hostility. Accordingly, in German eyes, he appeared as a mere shuffling tacticians Men like Field-Marshal Lord Milne[143] had seen the danger earlier and warned the English people that they were fighting an essentially unified force.

The abandonment, however, of the pretence that the German people were the unwilling, groaning slaves of Hitler—a pretence maintained so long and with such "damnable iteration,"[144] must have had a serious effect on the British "morale."

The man who had been taught that the purpose of the war was to save Polish integrity saw that it had been entirely lost. The man who had been taught to believe that, in the first few weeks of war, the German people would rise against Hitler was told, at this late hour, that they were just as bad as their leader, and solidly behind him. The man who had been waiting for revolutions in Austria and Czecho-Slovakia waited in vain.

Certainly a few revolutions were synthesized in the offices of Reuter[145] and Havas:[146] but the failure of neutral journalists to discover any sign of these insurrections created in English public opinion a stronger distrust of the Ministry of Information than had hitherto been entertained. Having been disappointed in so many respects, the British public waited for Germany's economic collapse, confidently expected in the first month of the war. It did not come. All the predictions of the Press seemed to be wrong.

Perhaps not all. Obscurely tucked away in the financial columns of the *News Chronicle* for November 22, 1938, is the following passage:

"The success of the last loan was greatly helped by the fact that before the lists were closed Hitler had 'pulled it off' at Munich. Whether the present issue will be equally successful remains to be seen. There is no

---

[143] Field Marshal George Francis Milne, (1866–1948), Chief of the Imperial General Staff from 1926 to 1933.

[144] O, thou hast damnable iteration, and art indeed able to corrupt a saint." William Shakespeare, *Henry IV,* Part 1, act 1, Scene 2.

[145] Paul Julius Freiherr von Reuter (1816–1899), a German-born Jew who founded the Reuters news agency.

[146] Charles-Louis Havas (1783–1858), a French-born Jew who founded a news agency named after him, which today is known as Agence France-Presse (AFP).

reason to suppose that it will not be, for everybody is now employed in Germany, saving is therefore proceeding at a fairly high rate and, which is most important, savings have practically no alternative outlet to Government loans. Many people express surprise that Germany can go on financing rearmament on the present huge scale of probably £ 800,000,000 a year. It cannot therefore be too strongly stressed that in a totalitarian state—or a well-run democratic state either—finance *per se* is not likely to break down. Provided the Government can produce sufficient consumable goods to feed and clothe its population adequately and can distribute sufficiently equitably what it does produce, finance can always be made to play its part. The last straw will certainly not be a financial one."

Information of this kind the *News Chronicle* kept for its investors. The ordinary readers just perused the prominently featured articles which predicted the economic collapse of Germany within a few months, and which declared that Hitler had cured unemployment only by putting all the unemployed into concentration camps.

The writer, of course, erred in suggesting that financial control was possible in a democratic state: but he had to say something in order to palliate a statement which would have drawn a howl of protest from the Jews, if it had been made without some qualification.

There were very few warnings of this kind: and today, with their own income tax at 7/6 in the pound, with their exports at 50 per cent of the pre-war figure, with more than 80 per cent of their foreign investments lost, with an increase of more than 20 per cent in prices, with a daily war expenditure of seven million pounds, the middle classes of Britain are still pathetically awaiting Germany's economic collapse, simply because they do not understand that in Germany goods rule money, and money does not rule goods.

The British Government made no bigger mistake than that of initiating against Germany a blockade of foodstuffs and other essential commodities. Here was another factor contributory to the shattering of the illusion that England's rulers were inspired with affection for the German working man.

The proposal to starve his wife and children into democracy was the surest method of demonstrating to the world the devotion which England's capitalist Government felt towards the working classes of other countries. From the outset, the attempt was doomed to failure. Germany's good understanding with Italy, Russia, Japan and many other countries made it possible to obtain overland a sufficient quantity of imports to render needless all anxiety as to the future. Moreover, her own production, so marvellously increased under National-Socialist rule, guaranteed her absolutely against starvation.

Even in petroleum, she has been able to produce a high proportion of her requirements at home: that is to say, she has been producing more than half of her ordinary peace-time needs in oil fuel. England's position has been very different.

The magnificent achievements of the German Fleet, in control of the North Sea, have rendered Britain's problem of imports more difficult each day. How desperate her position has become can be judged from her utterly illegal proposal to confiscate, wherever she can, any neutral goods that may have been acquired from Germany.

It is not surprising that both the U.S.A. and Russia replied to this manifesto in terms of cold contempt, and Japan in terms of hostility. The little countries, of course, like "gallant little Belgium" are proper to be bullied by a great democracy fighting for the welfare of small peoples.

When poor Belgium protested that her trade was being ruined by the blockade, she was told by some pompous Ass-In-Office, *Cross yclept*,[147] that her losses represented a very small contribution to the cause of saving democracy: to which the only appropriate answer is: "Haw! Haw!"[148]

Countries like Denmark and Holland have already, at the beginning of 1940, been ruined by the blockade: but if the women and children of every neutral state in the world were starving in the streets, their agony would still be only a small contribution to the smooth progress of Israel's chariots.

In England, however, the rising taxes, the rising prices, the wild confusion caused by evacuation, the commandeering of hotels, the collapse of the educational system, the daily blunders of the Ministry of Information, have led to the resignations of Lord Macmillan and Hore-Belisha from the Cabinet.

The former was just a poor Scottish lawyer, who found it against his nature to make lies out of truth and truth out of nothing. He was inefficient, and he went. Hore-Belisha, however, has been moved back even as the Knight to guard the King. Had the war gone well, his melon-

---

[147] *Ycelpt*: the past participle of *clepe*, from the Old English *clipian*, to speak, call.
148 This appears to be the first use of the phrase "Haw-Haw" by Joyce.

like physiognomy would have expanded in a horrible Moroccan Jewish grin: as, however, all seemed to be going badly, it was thought better by Jewry itself to withdraw him from the public gaze.

Chamberlain was tired of being told that his War Minister was an Oriental pedlar of furniture: and anti-Jewish feeling has been increasing to such an extent in England that J Division of the London Metropolitan Constabulary (Bethnal Green) had to be forbidden, in December 1939, to laugh at criticisms of the Jews expressed at public meetings.

It would have been contrary to the Army's traditions to issue an order requiring officers and other ranks to abstain from laughing at their Minister for War.

Yet there is no doubt that both laughter and disgust were occasioned by the funny antics of this shoving, pushing, self-advertising, gaudy, garish, clever little Jew-boy. His departure from the Cabinet meant no loss to Jewry: for Winston Spencer Churchill was there to hold the fort.

This illustrious descendant on his father's side of the famous Duke of Marlborough, became the kept protégé of Mr. Barney Baruch[149] some years ago.

His amazing tergiversations during the first decade of the century excited public contempt. He coined that most unfortunate phrase

---

149 Bernard Mannes Baruch (1870–1965), an American-born Jew who in 1916 became an official advisor to President Woodrow Wilson on national defense and terms of peace. He served on the Advisory Commission to the Council of National Defense and, in 1918, became the chairman of the new War Industries Board. When the United States entered World War II, President Roosevelt appointed Baruch a special adviser to the director of the Office of War Mobilization. Baruch had been personal friends with Churchill since 1917, when the latter was British Minister of Munitions and Baruch was in charge of munitions production in the US. Churchill was in Baruch's debt because he would have been bankrupted in the stock market crash of 1929. In that crash, Churchill had lost a significant amount of cash, and by coincidence was in North America on a lecture tour on the day that share prices went into free fall. As related in the book *Eleanor Roosevelt* Volume 2, by Blanche Wiesen Cook (Viking, 1999), after the crash of 1929, Churchill visited the New York Stock Exchange and decided to gamble as if he were in a casino. He did his betting in Baruch's office. At the end of the day, Churchill was in tears. He was, he said, a ruined man. Everything he owned, all his property, would have to be sold; he would even be forced to resign from the House of Commons. Baruch calmed him down. You haven't lost anything, he told him. As Churchill's biographer, William Manchester, relates, "Baruch had left instructions to buy every time Churchill sold and sell whatever Churchill bought. Winston had come out exactly even because, he later learned, Baruch even paid the commissions." Churchill later called Baruch his "favorite American."

"terminological inexactitude"[150] to palliate one of his own most blatant attempts at cheating the public. When Home Secretary in 1911, he showed his friendship for the workers by ordering the military to open fire on the miners of South Wales. Two were killed and many injured.[151]

During the last war, as First Lord of the Admiralty, he issued the report that the Battle of Jutland was lost. The markets crashed. In an ecstasy of patriotism, he and his comrades bought shares. Then he issued a second report. This time the Battle of Jutland was won.

The necessity to peg the market had now expired. Therefore he and his comrades sold what they had bought. That they made a vast profit was due to their skilful blending of patriotic self-sacrifice with commercial acumen.

Mr. Churchill's able leadership during the last war will be remembered by all those who lost their relations and friends in the holocaust of the Dardanelles,[152] so assiduously organized by this imitation strategist.

It was a significant omen that when he moved into the Admiralty in September 1939, he asked for the same furniture as he had had when he was previously Butcher-In-Chief to His Majesty the King. After the war, he wanted to send a military expedition against the Russians,

---

[150] "Terminological inexactitude" is a phrase introduced in 1906 by Churchill. Today, it is used as a euphemism or circumlocution meaning a lie or untruth. Churchill first used the phrase during the 1906 election. After the election in the House of Commons, as Under-Secretary of the Colonial Office, he repeated what he had said during the campaign: "The conditions of the Transvaal ordinance ... cannot in the opinion of His Majesty's Government be classified as slavery; at least, that word in its full sense could not be applied without a risk of terminological inexactitude." It seems this first usage was strictly literal, merely a roundabout way of referring to inexact or inaccurate terminology. But it was soon interpreted or taken up as a euphemism for an outright lie.

[151] The Welsh Miner's Riots of 1911 (sometimes known as the Rhondda Riots) was a series of violent confrontations between coal miners and police that took place at various locations in and around the Rhondda mines in south Wales. The riots were the culmination of an industrial dispute between workers and the mine owners. Home Secretary Winston Churchill's decision to allow troops to be sent to the area to reinforce the police shortly after the 8 November riot caused ill feeling towards him in south Wales throughout his life.

[152] The Gallipoli Campaign, also known as the Dardanelles Campaign, or the Battle of Gallipoli, was a major Allied defeat during the First World War. Drafted by Churchill in his role as First Lord of the Admiralty, it consisted of a major landing on Turkish soil on the Dardanelles peninsula with the eventual aim of capturing the Ottoman capital of Constantinople. The naval attack was repelled and, after eight months' fighting, with the Allied forces suffering massive casualties, the land campaign also failed and the invasion force was withdrawn to Egypt.

whom he characterized as "Bloody Baboons." During the earlier part of 1939, the amazing creature pleaded with tears in his voice for an alliance between Britain and Soviet Russia.

His personal habits are such that his chief following in England consists of unpaid tradesmen. So long as Winston Churchill has any part in the governance of Britain, so long can the fat creatures lolling in the tents of Israel feel that they are adequately represented by the first Honorary Jew in the world.

The term "Honorary," however, is not to be interpreted in its financial sense. What campaign he will stage to rival the futilities of the Dardanelles remains to be seen: but this much is certain: no living man bears so great a responsibility for the bloodshed of this war as this posturing lackey of Judah.

At the same time, no more fitting representative could be found for the rotten old system against which Germany has been compelled to fight. The thought of this rotten old system suggests the necessity for a final analysis of the principles at stake in this historic struggle.

To view the war as a mere combat between Germany on the one hand and the Allies on the other is natural from the pragmatic military point of view: but it is to lose sight of the greatest and most fundamental change that has come upon the human race since the Renaissance or even the collapse of the Roman Empire.

As Burke has written; "In politics magnanimity is often the truest wisdom." It is well, then, to realize that Jewish finance is as bent on the enslavement of the English people as of the German.

The military power of England, the spurious Jingoism engendered of the Jewish need for military defenders, the sacrifices of the British fighting forces all play their part today.

But, in the event of British victory, all this synthesized nationalism would be destroyed in a few months.

The supreme fact of world politics today is that the Jews want no nationalism but their very own. If an Englishman cannot fight in his own streets against the domination of international finance, it were better for him to go elsewhere and impede by every means in his power the victory of his Government: for the victory of such a Government would be the everlasting defeat of his race: it would put an end to all prospects for ever of social justice and fundamental economic reform. Of course, it is a mistake to regard the whole situation as a function of economics. No important historical situation has ever been such.

When Mussolini raised the standards of Fascism, long before his economic policy was understood or even properly formulated, he was assailed by Western Democracy as a scoundrel: for he had dared to assert the principle of authority. Such audacity was much to be feared.

Four hundred years ago, the Renaissance, with its bombardment of Greek philosophies, had brought in an era of doubt, philosophical and otherwise. In the world of science, this doubt proved of great advantage: in the world of politics and morals, it gradually degenerated into that negation of belief which paralyses all human action. Empires faded and monarchies crumbled.

Their dissolution seemed slow, because the germs of decay operated from within. Decades before their end came, they were doomed.

Autocracy as something above the people and not proceeding from them survived only in the hidden form of High Finance, which gilded every one of its nefarious acts with the name of liberty.

The last war brought the old gods down. Kaisers and Kings, Princes and Dukes faded away: and the Empire of the world was transferred to the counting houses. There the profit-makers had one sole aim—to make profit.

For them the science and the art of government had no significance apart from profits: all that they needed in the way of statecraft could be supplied by babbling democratic assemblies which threw up the facade of popular representation in order that the financiers might operate behind it.

To them, discipline and order seemed loathsome things—as loathsome as a well-ordered condition of the body would be to some noxious germ. The call to authority sounded to them like the knell of doom. Once men began to think again in terms of leadership, authority, discipline, unity, government would cease to serve a small class of financiers and begin to concern itself with the real welfare of the people.

When Adolf Hitler began to proclaim the principle of authority in Germany as the only condition of Germany's redemption from defeat, the horror of the democrats grew apace. He had committed the most unpardonable crime of perceiving the truth and stating it. He saw that the tasks of peace no less than those of war demand a leadership armed with the greatest power to act. That the people should choose their leaders was natural: but once chosen, they must rule; otherwise they would be useless. Here was a flagrant violation of democratic principle.

In the fashionable view, it was better for a hungry man without any money to look into a shop-window full of food than for him to be given work and mobilized under authority for the work of peace. This view was held by many people who had never been hungry in their lives. Many of them were so simple that they never thought of how many unpleasant orders have to be absolutely obeyed when they are given to a man by his employer.

The proprietor of a fish-and-chip shop can talk as he likes to his underlings, bully them, frighten them with the threat of dismissal, reduce their wages, decide when and how they are to work without at all impairing the glorious principle of liberty: but once let the ruler of a state who loves his people issue absolute orders for their own welfare, and he is denounced as a dictator—a tyrant.

Again, men of commerce who enforce the most stringent discipline in their own establishments, even dictating the kind of collar that their clerks should wear, throw up their hands in horror at the suggestion that the concerted management of the whole state requires even more discipline and control than they have to impose on a few hundred or a few thousand employees.

"The Boss's word is law" is an old principle in business. Why, then, should it be argued that the only business in which everybody should try to please himself is that of the state? The answer is that the people are easy to exploit, so long as they have no consciousness of their own organic unity.

Thus, the dynamic development of evolution renders the totalitarian state essential to the existence of those great, modern peoples who have become associated with what is called industry.

An island with only one inhabitant, cut off from the rest of the world, would be a perfect democracy. The population could do as it pleased, so long as it did not die of starvation. If two people had to live on the island, unless they never saw each other, problems might arise as to how much each could please himself.

If the population rose to ten thousand, and the island had an area of only one square mile, the amount of individual liberty would have to be greatly diminished. Either authority, anarchy, or rotten government would prevail.

But when fifty million people live on an island, when the majority of them have no direct contact with the primary production of essential commodities and have to depend for their livelihood on a complicated network of relationships, it is clear that only the sternest authority, and an authority above partisan disputes, can protect the welfare of the greatest numbers.

In such a society, the question is not how much individual liberty a man can possess, but rather how much he should resign in order to make life tolerable for himself and for others.

Until the last few years, it was thought that this gigantic problem could best be solved by "laissez-faire," those who possessed the most money calmly buying the liberty of others. Hence the striking difference between the liberty of the millionaire and that of the coal miner.

The theory has had a long run: but it was bound to be abandoned somewhere and by somebody.

In Germany it has been replaced by the theory of the totalitarian state. This theory, so cursed by the democracies, simply means that every living being in the state, instead of being allowed to rot of money or of starvation, is integrated into the organic whole of the community.

The poorer people, so long regarded as a sloughing ulcer, become a healthy member of the body. The conception is merely in accord with the teaching of science and the laws of nature.

In nature, a system of relations impeded by an unorganized mass in its midst is a monstrosity, something worse than the most hideous function.

Indeed, if we draw upon pathology for an example, we may say that when a part of the body falls out of its proper and clearly established relation with the whole, both the part and the whole become diseased.

In nature, moreover, there is no democracy. As the *Gestalt* psychologists[153] and the best physicists have shown, in any entity composed of systems of relations, there must be a super-relation integrating all the other systems, over and above them.

A tune is not the sum of a number of notes: the melody is determined by the relation between the notes: but the tune as a whole derives its ultimate character from the totalitarian and organic integration of the different parts of the melody. The last note, for example, of the *Last Post* stands not only in relation to the preceding note but to the whole tune.

---

[153] The concept of *gestalt* was first introduced in philosophy and psychology in 1890 by the Austrian philosopher Christian von Ehrenfels (1859–1932). *Gestalt* psychology or *gestaltism* (German: *Gestalt* "shape, form") holds that the mind forms a global whole with self-organizing tendencies. This principle maintains that when the human mind (perceptual system) forms a percept or *gestalt*, the whole has a reality of its own, independent of the parts.

In the same way, a human being's will, character, and personality stand over and above all mere relations between physical and mental acts, though all such acts are brought into relationship with the whole being, unless such pathological developments as amnesia or split personality should unfortunately make their appearance.

In fact, it is not possible to conceive any system of relations ungoverned by a superior relation between all the parts of the thing concerned: and, so far as human organization is concerned, integration of desires and sentiments throughout a community can be effected only by undivided will and undivided personality representative not necessarily in the intellectual but certainly in the volitional and emotional sense of the whole.

No man in his senses would suggest that questions of chemistry and physiology should be decided by popular vote. Even a jury of 12 supposedly intelligent persons is more apt to be confused than enlightened by the clash of expert opinion in Court: and the usual course is to lean entirely on the Learned Judge's opinion after the experts have done their damnedest.

But is it not a mistake to suppose that problems of statecraft are necessarily more simple than those of chemistry or physiology? At any rate, the scope for dangerous generalizations and loose thinking is far wider: and the subjective element of prejudice is far stronger.

Thus, in the complex conditions of modern life, at least, an intellectual democracy is utterly beyond attainment.

There can be no right judgement without sound data: and the claim that the public always has all the necessary data upon which to decide all problems of state cannot be sustained.

On the other hand, as is shown in National Socialist Germany, the will and feeling of a whole nation can be expressed in the personality of one man.

The man is Adolf Hitler: and even his worst enemies have had to admit that it is useless to try to make distinctions between him and his people.

In this respect, as in all others, he differs from the leaders of the democracies, who have to lie most ingeniously to keep their precarious positions. The German Führer is thus that super-relationship which gives final expression and direction to the unity of the German Nation. Yet the system is such that, inestimable though his loss to Germany would be, another leader would emerge in the tragic event of his death.

From the viewpoint of the worker, the most important aspect of the totalitarian state to remember is the fact that its organic nature does not permit the existence of floating masses of poor and unemployed outside the structure of society. Every single worker knows and feels his relationship to the state as a whole. He knows his rights as well as his duties. He knows that he cannot get out of the state what he fails to put into the state: but he also knows that what he does put in, he will get back in full measure.

The German worker is enabled by the State to take wonderful holidays: he can cruise to Madeira: he can go to the best opera in the world: he can enjoy himself at winter sports: indeed it is no exaggeration to say that the rich have no pleasures which have not been put at his disposal.

Poor there still are: nor would any reasonable person suppose that all hardship could be eliminated in six years: but anybody who has seen the Winter Help Work[154] in progress must admire the marvellous spirit in which it is conducted. Those who need assistance do not have to ask for it. It is pressed upon them. Through the functioning of the National Socialist Welfare Organization all the miserable formalities associated with relief schemes in other countries are avoided: and where the poor in Germany need help they get it, not as a form of charity, but as a simple act of comradely duty altogether implicit in the structure of the state. This is a simple illustration of what totalitarianism means.

The totalitarian organization of industry has, for all practical purposes, abolished unemployment. Indeed, even before this war, Germany had to' import labour.

Let us draw a picture, for a moment. A man is sitting in a cold, drab, bare room in the early winter afternoon. He is looking at his wife with impatience. She, poor wretch, is looking at him with hopelessness and secretly wondering why she married him, great though her sympathy with him may be. Two children in rags, their eyes red with crying for food, are whimpering in a corner over the tattered body of a decrepit doll. A quarter loaf of stale bread is on the table: and the icy rain is

---

[154] The Winterhilfswerk (English: Winter Relief, lit. "winter help work") was an annual drive by the Nationalsozialistische Volkswohlfahrt (National Socialist People's Welfare Organization) to help finance charitable work. Its slogan was "None shall starve nor freeze". It ran from 1933 to 1945 during the months of October through March, and was designed to provide food, clothing, coal, and other items to less fortunate Germans during the inclement months. Similar initiatives were started in countries in German-occupied Europe, known in French as the *Secours d'Hiver* and in Dutch as the *Winterhulp*.

beating on the windows. He has been out all morning looking for work. The tentative promise made to him has broken down. For the hundredth time in six months, he has given that savage shake of the head to his wife on entering the little home, where they had a turkey and some wine the Christmas before last.

There are no pictures of this kind in Germany today. I have seen many in England. You may think that you can understand the mental processes of that man and woman. Unless you have been poor, you cannot. You can no more understand them than you could understand the mental processes of a cat that you had found with a broken leg and taken to the animals' hospital to be cured.

What matters, in such a case, is not the poverty of the moment, not the shortage of food, but the feeling that it will always be so, as long as body and soul keep precariously together. Worse even than that is the feeling of the man who has mental or physical ability, but whom society does not want and who knows that society does not want him.

Here is your unrelated fragment. Nothing that he can do, nothing that he can say, nothing that he can suffer, be he endowed with the strength of a Titan,[155] the skill of a Paganini,[156] the intellect of a Newton,[157] nothing, nothing can bring him into relation with a society that does not want him. He is free to rot amidst the blessings of democracy. He is free because he is just a little wart on the body politic. If he was formerly a professional man or a clerk, he gets nothing. If he was a manual labourer, he may get hurled at him just enough to sustain consciousness in his miserable condition.

The wisest words on this subject were written by Thomas Carlyle:

"*Liberty?* The true liberty of a man you would say consists in his finding out, or being forced to find out, the right path   and to walk thereon. To learn or to be taught what work he actually was able for, and then by permission, persuasion, and even compulsion, to set about doing of the same. That is the true blessedness, hondur, 'liberty'

---

[155] In Classical Greek mythology, the Titans were members of the second order of divine beings, descending from the primordial deities and preceding the Olympian deities. They were giant deities of incredible strength, who ruled during the legendary Golden Age, and also composed the first pantheon of Greek deities.

[156] Niccolò Paganini (1782–1840), an Italian violinist, violist, guitarist, and composer. He was the most celebrated violin virtuoso of his time, and left his mark as one of the pillars of modern violin technique.

[157] Sir Isaac Newton (1642–1726), an English physicist and mathematician who is widely recognised as one of the most influential scientists of all time and as a key figure in the scientific revolution.

and maximum of well-being. If liberty be not that, I for one have small care about liberty."[158]

Thomas Carlyle was a great National-Socialist: and Germany has repaid him for his scholarship on her behalf by honouring his philosophy when it is scorned in Britain.

Another great division between National-Socialist Germany and the old world is its ruthless rejection of materialism. The cardinal philosophical principle of National-Socialism is the belief, as the guiding principle of life, in the transcendental ability of the human, non-material will, to overcome all material obstacles and to make environment the slave of human personality.

Oddly enough, it is Carlyle again who has inimitably expressed the spirit of Germany today.

He writes: "It is a calumny on men to say that they are roused to a heroic action by ease, hope of pleasure, recompense—a sugar plum of any kind in this world or the next. In the meanest mortal there is something nobler. The poor swearing soldier, hired to be shot, has his 'honour of a soldier' different from drill regulations and the shilling a day. It is not to taste sweet things, but to do noble and true things, and vindicate himself under God's Heaven as a god-made man, that the poorest son of Adam dimly longs. Show him the way of doing that, and the dullest day-drudge becomes a hero. They wrong man greatly who say he is to be seduced by ease. Difficulty, abnegation, martyrdom, death, are the allurements that act on the heart of man. Kindle the inner genial life of him, you have a flame that burns up all lower considerations."[159]

That "genial" life has been kindled in the German man by Adolf Hitler: and the flame will be borne in triumph from generation to generation "to the last syllable of recorded time."[160]

National-Socialism gives the worker rights to defend. It gives every worker the knowledge that he is an honoured and integral part of the state. It lays great emphasis on providing him with all that the earth can yield: but the greatest emphasis is ever on the spiritual truth that survival is an act, not of digestion, but of will.

Thus, whilst assured of all that his land's resources can offer, he is prepared to sacrifice all, that his children may advance one stage further along the road of civilization. The old squabbles about private

---

[158] Thomas Carlyle, *Past and Present*, Chap. 3.13 (1843).

[159] Thomas Carlyle, *On Heroes, Hero-worship and the Heroic in History.* (1841).

[160] Shakespeare: *Macbeth*, Act 5, Scene 5.

property, surplus values, and the like have no meaning in National-Socialist Germany. When the state can assure an equitable distribution of private property, very few people are likely to object to private property as an institution.

For the same reason, class war has vanished. There can be no class war in a genuine totalitarian state.

So much has been written about totalitarianism, because many honest people in England consider it the main difference between England and Germany. Ultimately, it is a tremendous difference, but not enough to cause a war by itself.

That the British democracy has no objection to dictatorship is shown by its adulation of the black Dictator, Haile Selassie,[161] its admiration for Dollfuss, who ruled by sheer military force, its undying, if ineffectual love for Benesh, Beck, and Smygly-Ridz, and its untiring but unsuccessful wooing of Stalin.

If Adolf Hitler would accept the system of international finance and the Jews associated with it, there would be peace in ten minutes after his acceptance had been announced. Indeed, at the Mansion House,[162] on January 9, 1940, Mr. Chamberlain stated his real aim as the extension of Anglo-French financial cooperation to other countries of Europe and "possibly the whole world."

However, even if Hitler were prepared, as he never could be, to surrender his economic policy, he could not. For the great philosophical gap which I have indicated would render its resurgence a mere matter of months.

We have come, after these laborious centuries of groping, to the greatest turning point in world history.

In general, man is free to mould his destiny: but there are exceptions. To study the career of that simple man, Adolf Hitler, to weigh his words, to observe his actions is to know that he alone of all the German people, is the least free: for he is the servant of a Higher Destiny. A survey of the facts given in this book should show that even if he had never been born, the old system of International Finance must have rushed to its doom; even as the merchant princes realized that science had

---

[161] Haile Selassie I (1892–1975), dictator regent of Ethiopia from 1916 to 1930 and Emperor of Ethiopia from 1930 to 1974. As the author of this book correctly points out, the "democracies" of Britain and France had no problem with "autocratic" rule in Ethiopia, and lauded Selassie as a hero.
[162] Mansion House is the official home and office of the Lord Mayor of the City of London.

abolished time and distance, they would have sought out the cheapest labour in the world and left the white populations starving, whilst the coloured slaves did the work.

The full selfishness of the whole system was about to produce its own fatal consequences, when war was declared on Germany in the vain hope of giving it a new lease of life.

Yet, it is a merciful dispensation of Providence that, in Nature's progress, the principle of destruction has never finished its dire work before the principle of construction appears.

In metabolism, the breakdown of cells without their replacement means atrophy and death: and if the Good God had meant the world to die in these years, He would have entrusted its extermination to some force more in keeping with His nobility than the Jewish race.

Just as the old world, then, was crumbling, the new force of construction arose in the person of Hitler and the body of the Third Reich. There are millions of men and women today, young in mind and spirit, who cannot accept the gloomy fatalism of Spengler.[163]

There is, despite all corruption enough eternal youth left in the world to fight to the last against the doctrine of despair. To those who preach decline and decay, there is the answer of indomitable National-Socialist challenge.

The men who rule England are old: the class that holds supremacy is tarnished and decayed: there is much demoralization among the British people: but the pulse of historic youth still beats, however faintly.

Devoted as I am, with undivided allegiance to my new home for the rest of my life, I hope and pray that this pulse, so feeble now, will quicken into vitality, and one day throb with life.

When the smoke of battle has rolled away, when those of us who are left, gaze on the cold ashes of the conflagration started on that bright September morning by the bankrupt politicians of Britain, when we count the toll of life that war has taken, when we think of the misery that it has inflicted on the millions, when we smile grimly on the charred fragments of what was once the Power of Judah, when the glory of the ancient gods has crumbled to the dust from which it came, the birth pangs of the new order will be over. Throughout the whole of his life as a Leader, Adolf Hitler, has shown his love for the working people: he

---

[163] *The Decline of the West* (German: "Der Untergang des Abendlandes"), is a two-volume work by German philosopher Oswald Spengler (1880–1936), first published in 1918. In this famous work, Spengler argues that the Western world is ending and is witnessing the last season — "winter time" — of the Faustian civilization.

has offered England the hand of friendship till it could be spurned no more. In the days of his inevitable victory, when Britain is freed from the forces of darkness that have caused this war, the defeat of England will be her victory.

To, achieve their regeneration, her people will have to suffer much: and the longer the war lasts, the more they will have to suffer: but they will have the chance, so long denied to them, of using their genius and their character in the building of that new world to which Adolf Hitler has shown the way.

In these days, it may be presumptuous to express either hopes or beliefs: yet I will venture so much. I hope and believe, that when the flames of war have been traversed, the ordinary people of England will know their soul again and will seek, in National-Socialism, to advance along the way of human progress in friendship with their brothers of German blood.

That this hope and this belief shall not prove vain there are two guarantees, for me sufficient; the greatness of Adolf Hitler and the Greater Glory of Almighty God.

Index

R

Randlords 116
Reuter, Paul Julius Freiherr von 154
Rothschild, Nathan Mayer, Freiherr von 26
Rothschilds 26, 52, 78, 99, 102, 107, 124
Rousseau, Jean-Jacques 42
Rydz-Śmigły, Marshal Edward 149, 150

S

Sadowa, Battle of 31
Samuel, Marcus 64
Sassoon, Sir Philip 52, 66, 67, 106, 110
Scanlon, John 43, 129
Schiff, Jacob 130
Schuschnigg, Kurt Alois Josef Johann 140
Schuster, Sir Felix 66, 94, 122, 124
Scottish Life Assurance 95
Scottish Nationalism 117
Second Anglo-Boer War 113
Selfridge's 109
Shakespeare, William 39, 93, 154, 166
Shawcross, Sir Hartley 3
Sieff, Israel Moses 99, 100, 101, 104, 105
Siegfried Line 150
Snowden, Philip 48
Spectator 104
Spengler, Oswald 168
Speyer, Sir Edgar 32
Stalin 146, 167
St. Ignatius Loyola 1
Stock Exchange 27, 36, 43, 45, 49, 104, 157
Stock Exchange Year-book 104
Streseman, Gustav 132
Strike of 1926 47, 61
Stuart, Charles 14, 15, 33, 37
Sudeten Germans 141
Sudetenland 141, 142
Suez canal 32
Sunday Dispatch 105, 106
Sunday Express 71, 108
Sunday Pictorial 70, 104
Swift, Jonathan 16

T

Tatler 104
"Terminological inexactitude" 40, 158
Thomas, James Henry "Jimmy" 49
Timbuctoo 134
The Times 59, 73, 96, 102, 109, 125, 140
Treaty of Versailles 129, 130
Trevelyan, G.M. 19

U

Unilever 95
University of London 4

V

Versailles 31, 53, 129, 130, 132, 133, 139, 141—144
Vikings 38, 157

W

Wagner 9
Waley-Cohen, Sir Robert 64, 102
Walpole, Robert 16
Wandsworth Prison 3
Waterloo, Battle of 26, 91
Waugh, Alec 131
Weizmann, Chaim 50, 106, 124, 126
Welsh Miner's Riots of 1911 158
Wentworth, Thomas, Earl of Strafford 12
Whigs 14, 15, 16, 17, 19
Whitehall 46, 61, 117, 118, 145, 146
White-slave traffic 104
William, Prince of Orange 15
Williams Deacons bank 65
Wilson, Woodrow 37, 130, 133, 157
Winterhilfswerk 164
Woolworths 99, 100

Z

Zangwill, Israel 86
Zinoviev letter 46
Zionist seizure of Palestine 114
Zollvereine 31

Lightning Source UK Ltd.
Milton Keynes UK
UKHW022338040520
362767UK00019B/3936